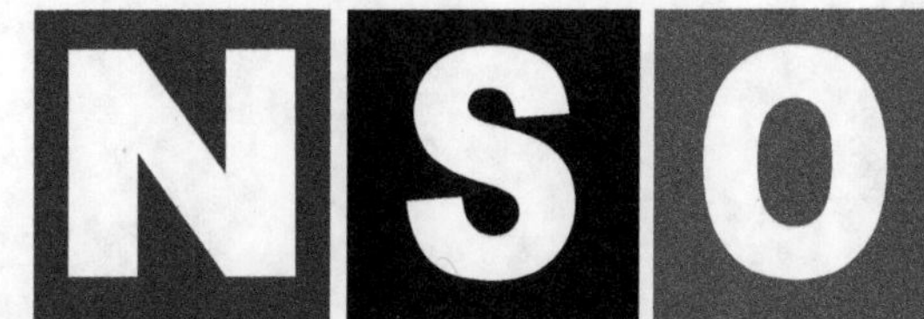

OLYMPIAD WORKBOOK

NATIONAL SCIENCE OLYMPIAD

- **01** Learning Objectives
- **02** Multiple Choice Questions
- **03** HOTS (Achievers Section)
- **04** Model Test Paper
- **05** Answer Keys and Solutions
- **06** OMR Answer Sheet

V&S PUBLISHERS

Published by:

V&S PUBLISHERS

F-2/16, Ansari road, Daryaganj, New Delhi-110002
☎ 23240026, 23240027 • *Fax:* 011-23240028
✉ info@vspublishers.com • 🌐 www.vspublishers.com

Online Brandstore: amazon.in/vspublishers

Regional Office : Hyderabad
5-1-707/1, Brij Bhawan (Beside Central Bank of India Lane)
Bank Street, Koti, Hyderabad - 500 095
☎ 040-24737290
✉ vspublishershyd@gmail.com

Follow us on:   

BUY OUR BOOKS FROM: | AMAZON | | FLIPKART |

© Copyright: *V&S* PUBLISHERS
ISBN 978-81-977761-6-8
New Edition

PUBLISHER'S NOTE

V&S Publishers has carved a significant niche in the publishing industry over the last decade, having successfully published more than 1000 titles across 9 languages spanning over 50 subject categories. Being known for the quality of content, we have built a reputation of excellence and reliability. We have consistently delivered **"Value & Substance"** to our readers, through a wide range of titles across a variety of genres covering school books, fiction and non-fiction that caters to different people from every section of the society.

The **Olympiad Guidebooks for classes 1-10** across all subjects, launched almost a decade ago, under the **GEN X Imprint**, became a go-to-source for the school students in no time, owing to their invaluable and substantive content written in a guidebook pattern,.

Having successfully sold a million copies of the same and in response to demand by both students as well as shopkeepers nationwide; we now present before you our newly launched **Olympiad Workbook Series**, designed for **classes 1-10 across 4 subjects**.

The workbooks are meticulously curated by a team of experienced educators, researchers and subject matter experts, edited by professionals and peer reviewed by teachers. The team has poured its efforts and expertise into creating a crisp and concise workbook which will help and guide the students to the path of success in Olympiad exams. The **MCQs** identified will not only help in scoring top marks in Olympiads but also inculcate a sense of deeper understanding of the subject, by way of solving **HOTS** and referring to complete solutions at the end of the book.

Here we present our new release– **OLYMPIAD WORKBOOK (NSO) CLASS–1** having following features:

☞ Based on the latest syllabi

☞ MCQs with comprehensive coverage of topics

☞ HOTS Questions liberally included

☞ A dedicated chapter on logical reasoning

☞ Model test paper for thorough practice

☞ Sample OMR sheet for real time simulation

We have made sure through our best efforts, that this workbook strictly follows the latest syllabi and patterns of the Olympiad Examination.

As **V&S Publishers** continuously strive to enhance the readability and maintain the credibility of our academic publications, we seek the support of our valuable readers in influencing and enriching the lives of future generations of students.

P.S. While every care has been taken to ensure the correctness of the content, if you come across any error, howsoever minor, do not hesitate to discuss with teachers while pointing that out to us in no uncertain terms.

We wish you all the best for your exams!

DISTINCTIVE FEATURES

01 — Learning Objectives

They list the whole chapter as subtopics, helping the teachers to guide children in a step-by-step manner.

02 — Multiple Choice Questions

MCQs act as an excellent learning aid, helping you to understand and work on your mistakes.

03 — HOTS (Achievers Section)

The High Order Thinking Questions aim to help the student to solve Application-based questions and gain practical understanding of the subject.

04 — Model Test Paper

Model test paper are provided at the end of each book, which help the student to test the knowledge which they have gained after thorough reading of all chapters.

05 — Answer Key

Detailed Answer Key along with explanations aid the pupil to indentify, understand the mistakes they make during the course of Olympiad preparation.

CONTENTS

LIVING AND NON-LIVING THINGS

LEARNING OBJECTIVES

➤ Living and non-living things
➤ Characteristics of living things
➤ Natural and man-made things

MULTIPLE CHOICE QUESTIONS

Direction: Select the correct alternative from the given options.

1. Which of the following characteristic(s) belongs to both plants and animals?
   i. Need food and water to stay alive
   ii. Can respond to environmental change
   iii. Can move from one place to other by themselves
   iv. Reproduce
   (A) i, ii and iv only
   (B) i and ii only
   (C) iii only
   (D) i, ii and iii only

2. All non-living things have which of following characteristic(s)?
   (A) They need food to grow
   (B) They can respond to changes around them
   (C) They have offsprings
   (D) They might have been made from things that were once alive

3. Which of the following thing(s) can grow?

i. 

ii. 

iii. 

iv. 

   (A) i and ii   (B) i and iii
   (C) iii and iv   (D) i and iv

4. Which of the following group of things is obtained from living things?
   (A) Bark, hair, paper, tile
   (B) Bone, glass, sap, wood
   (C) Cotton, clay, leaf, milk
   (D) Cane, leather, silk, wool

5. Which of the following statements is not correct?
   (A) Suchit: Non-living things do not grow.
   (B) Shubhi: Non-living things cannot feel.

(C) Ananya: Non-living things do not breathe.

(D) Akash: Non-living things produce their offspring.

6. Match column I with column II and choose the correct option:

Column I	Column II
a. I am a man-made thing	i. 
b. I am a natural thing	ii.
c. I need oxygen to live	iii.
d. I need carbon dioxide to grow	iv.

(A) a-ii, b-i, c-iv, d-iii

(B) a-i, b-ii, c-iii, d-iv

(C) a-iii, b-i, c-iv, d-ii

(D) a-iv, b-i, c-ii, d-iii

7. Study the following diagrams.

i.   ii.   iii.   iv.

Which of the following need air, food and water to stay alive?

(A) i and iv only

(B) ii and iv only

(C) ii and iii only

(D) iii and iv only

8. Sanchit observes an unknown thing that moves, grows and reproduces. What did he conclude about it?

(A) It is a man-made thing.

(B) It is a non-living thing.

(C) It is alive and a living thing.

(D) It is a plant.

9. Which of the following groups contains only non-living things in an environment?

(A)

(B)

(C)

(D)

10. Which of the following statements describes that animals and plants respire?

i. Animals take in carbon dioxide and give out oxygen.

ii. Animals take in oxygen and give out carbon dioxide.

iii. Plants take in carbon dioxide and give out oxygen.

iv. Plants take in oxygen and give out carbon dioxide.

(A) i and iii only

(B) i and iv only

(C) ii and iii only

(D) ii and iv only

11. Identify the thing that does not need food and water.

(A) 
(B)
(C) 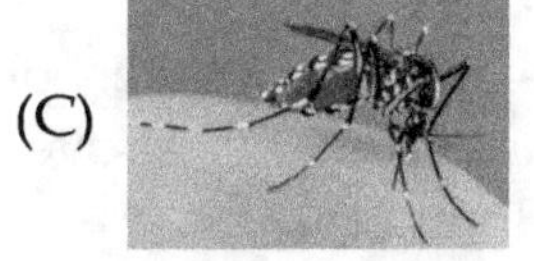
(D) 

12. Look at the car below.

The car shown above can move from one place to another but still it is a non-living thing because it __________.
(A) Cannot grow
(B) Feels
(C) Needs air to survive
(D) Requires food

13. Somya picked up a dry leaf. Her mother said it was a non-living thing because it __________.

   i.   Cannot move on its own
   ii. Cannot grow anymore
   iii. Cannot breathe anymore

(A) i and ii only
(B) i and iii only
(C) i, ii and iii only
(D) ii and iii only

14. Which one of the following groups is classified correctly?

Group	Living Thing	Non-Living Thing
(A)	Cow	Calf
(B)	Wooden table	Chair
(C)	Coconut tree	Plucked fruit
(D)	Dried leaf	Vase

15. Look at the following pictures and choose the correct option that correlates the following set of images:

(A) Can give birth to their young ones.
(B) Living things eat only grass.
(C) Need air, food and water.
(D) Can respond to changes around them.

16. Match the column (I) with Column (II).

Column I		Column II	
A.	Aeroplane	1.	Air, Water & Food
B.	Non-living things	2.	Non-living things
C.	Living thing needs	3.	Table

(A) A-3, B-2, C-1
(B) A-2, B-1, C-3
(C) A-2, B-3, C-1
(D) A-1, B-2, C-3

17. Consider the following statement and choose the correct answers.

Statement A: Table can move so it is a living thing.

Statement B: A plant is a living thing because it can grow.

(A) Statement 'A' is true and Statement 'B' is false.

(B) Statement 'B' is true and Statement 'A' is false.

(C) Both the statement are true.

(D) Both the statements are false.

18. Which of the following groups refers only to non-living things?

(A) Table, Aeroplane, Plants

(B) Teddy bear, Chair, Fan

(C) Plant, Cow, Aeroplane

(D) Birds, Plants, Cat

19. Book, flowers, cars, aeroplane, plant, table, chair, birds. From the above list. identify the non-living things.

(A) Birds, Flower, Table

(B) Plants, Aeroplane, Car

(C) Table, Chair, Aeroplane

(D) Flowers, Chair, Birds

20. Read the sentence carefully and find True (T) and False (F).

i. Living things needs air, water and food to grow.

ii. Plants are living things and aeroplane is a non-living thing.

iii. A chair can move by its own, it is a living thing.

(A) TFT
(B) TTT
(C) TTF
(D) FTP

1.	Ⓐ Ⓑ Ⓒ Ⓓ	5.	Ⓐ Ⓑ Ⓒ Ⓓ	9.	Ⓐ Ⓑ Ⓒ Ⓓ	13	Ⓐ Ⓑ Ⓒ Ⓓ	17.	Ⓐ Ⓑ Ⓒ Ⓓ
2.	Ⓐ Ⓑ Ⓒ Ⓓ	6.	Ⓐ Ⓑ Ⓒ Ⓓ	10.	Ⓐ Ⓑ Ⓒ Ⓓ	14.	Ⓐ Ⓑ Ⓒ Ⓓ	18.	Ⓐ Ⓑ Ⓒ Ⓓ
3.	Ⓐ Ⓑ Ⓒ Ⓓ	7.	Ⓐ Ⓑ Ⓒ Ⓓ	11.	Ⓐ Ⓑ Ⓒ Ⓓ	15.	Ⓐ Ⓑ Ⓒ Ⓓ	19.	Ⓐ Ⓑ Ⓒ Ⓓ
4.	Ⓐ Ⓑ Ⓒ Ⓓ	8.	Ⓐ Ⓑ Ⓒ Ⓓ	12.	Ⓐ Ⓑ Ⓒ Ⓓ	16.	Ⓐ Ⓑ Ⓒ Ⓓ	20.	Ⓐ Ⓑ Ⓒ Ⓓ

LEARNING OBJECTIVES

- ➤ Types of plants
- ➤ Where do plants come from?
- ➤ Parts of a plant
- ➤ Sources of food

MULTIPLE CHOICE QUESTIONS

Direction: Select the correct alternative from the given options.

1. Which of these is not a plant product?
   (A) Cabbage   (B) Almond
   (C) Egg   (D) Spinach

2. Which of these juices is extracted from the stem of a plant?
   (A) Orange juice
   (B) Sugarcane juice
   (C) Mango juice
   (D) All of these

3. Which of these is not a cereal?
   (A) Wheat
   (B) Lentil
   (C) Rice
   (D) Corn

4. Oil is extracted from which of the following plants?
   (A) Soyabean
   (B) Mustard
   (C) Groundnut
   (D) All of these

5. Which of these is made of coconut fibre?
   (A) Cloth
   (B) Coir mattress
   (C) Foam mattress
   (D) None of these

6. Which part of the plant makes food for the plant?
   (A) Stem
   (B) Flower
   (C) Leaves
   (D) Roots

7. Which of the following does not produce seeds?

   (A) 
   Banana

   (B) 
   Mango

   (C) 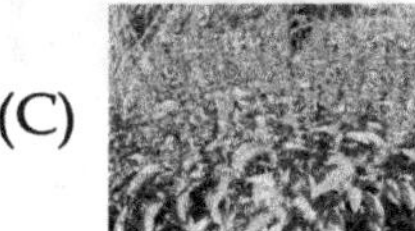
   Tulsi

   (D) 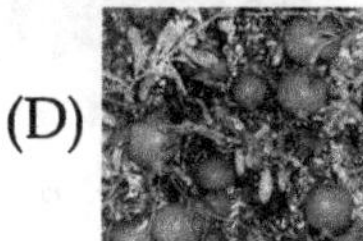
   Pomegranate

8. Match the leaf given below with its fruits.

   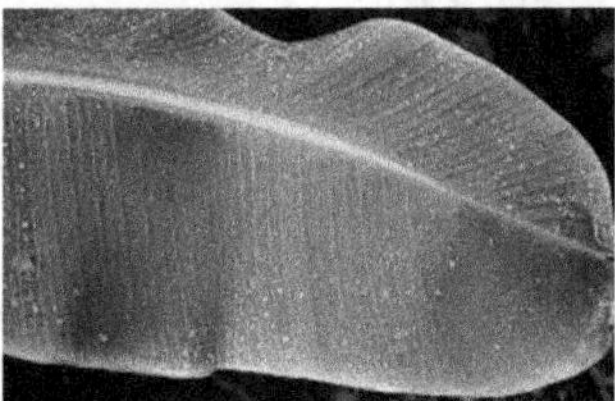

   (A) Mango   (B) Apple
   (C) Orange   (D) Banana

9. Which of the following is not a fruit?

(A) 
Brinjal

(B) 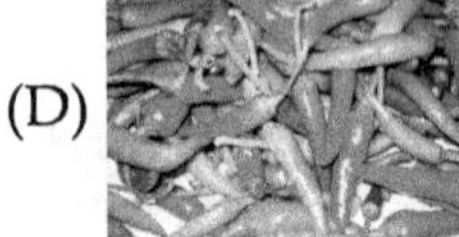
Lady Finger

(C) 
Onion

(D) 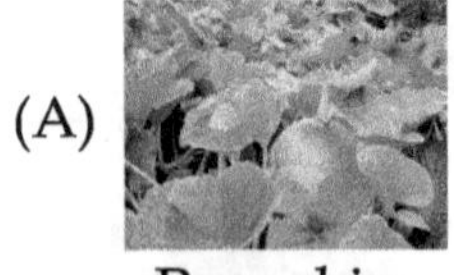
Chilli

10. Which of the following is a creeper?

(A) 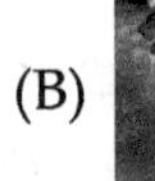
Pumpkin

(B) 
Money Plant

(C) 
Onion

(D) 
Grapes

11. Select the odd one out.

(A) 
Carrot

(B) 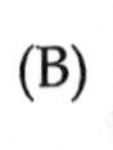
Turnip

(C) 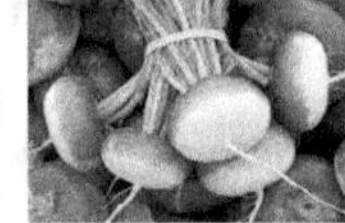
Radish

(D) 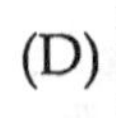
Pea plant

12. Which of these do we get from climbers?
(A) Cucumber
(B) Peas
(C) Watermelon
(D) Corn

13. Which of these flowers grow on a shrub?

(A) 
Gulmohar

(B) 
Rose

(C) 
Lotus

(D) 
Sunflower

14. Potato and sweet potato are ________.
(A) Leaves   (B) Stems
(C) Seeds   (D) Flowers

15. Tea and coffee are ________.
(A) Fruits
(B) Vegetables
(C) Plantation crops
(D) Stems

16. What will happen if we pick almost all flowers from the tree?
(A) Leaves will fall down
(B) Growth of the tree will be affected
(C) Less flowers means less seeds
(D) The tree will die

17. Which of the following statements is correct?
(A) Mango has many seeds
(B) Papaya has only one seed
(C) Wheat and rice are cereals
(D) Lentil is a cereal

18. Carefully look at the given flowchart. Which of the following can correctly fill the empty box of the flowchart?

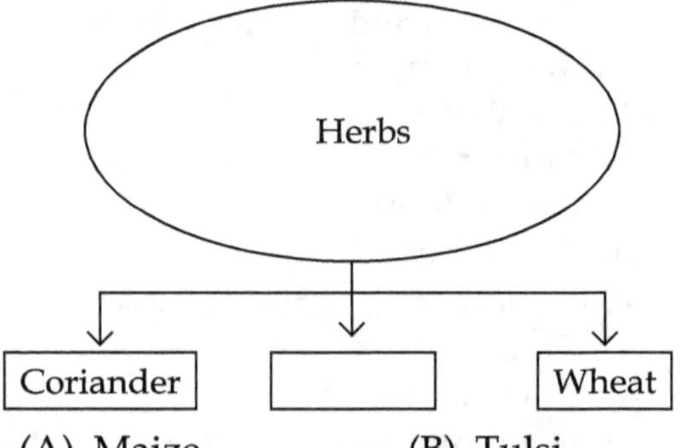

(A) Maize   (B) Tulsi
(C) Sugarcane   (D) Cotton

19. Which is this plant?

    (A) Papaya
    (B) Mango
    (C) Rose
    (D) Hibiscus

20. We eat the seeds of __________.

    (A) Turnip   (B) Corn
    (C) Banana   (D) Grapes

21. Which type of plants have the shortest life?

    (A) Tree   (B) Herb
    (C) Shrub   (D) Cactus

22. Which of these is not a woody tree used for making furniture?

(A) 
Teak

(B) 
Sal

(C) 
Rosewood

(D) 
Apple

23. This is a flower but it also gives us _______.

    (A) Fruits
    (B) Vegetables
    (C) Oil
    (D) Paper

24. Which of these is not a plant?

    (A) Wool
    (B) Jute
    (C) Cotton
    (D) Jute and cotton both

25. Which one of the following consists of plants with edible underground stems?

    (A) Ginger, garlic, potato, and onion
    (B) Turnip, tapioca, radish, and ginseng
    (C) Carrot, sweet potato, tapioca, and ginger
    (D) Water chestnut, peanut, walnut, and hazelnut

HOTS (ACHIEVERS SECTION)

26. Read the following conversation among four friends. Select the correct match of the child with different types of plants.

    Amit: They have thick stem. It is not as thick as the stems of trees. They are generally low in height.

    Shanu: They have soft green stems. They may live only one season. They are used for food, flavouring, medicine, or perfume.

    Somya: They have weak stems. The stems of these plants grow along the ground.

    Shruti: They have weak stems. The stems of these plants cannot grow without any support.

Child	Type of Plant
a. Amit	i. Climbers
b. Shanu	ii. Herbs
c. Somya	iii. Creepers
d. Shruti	iv. Shrubs

    (A) a-iv, b-ii, c-iii, d-i
    (B) a-iv, b-iii, c-ii, d-i
    (C) a-iii, b-i, c-ii, d-iv
    (D) a-ii, b-iv, c-iii, d-i

27. Look at the picture carefully.

Now read the following sentences and match I, II, III, and IV with the correct parts of the plant labels shown in the image (1, 2, 3, and 4).

I. Which part of the plant produces seeds and form new plants?

II. Which part of the plant makes the food for the plant? They take the water and mineral salts and use them together with sunlight and carbon dioxide to make food.

III. Which part of a plant is like the straw? It helps to move water around in the plant. It raises the leaves and flowers of the plant off the ground.

IV. Which part of a plant takes in water and mineral salts from the soil? They anchor the plant into the ground.

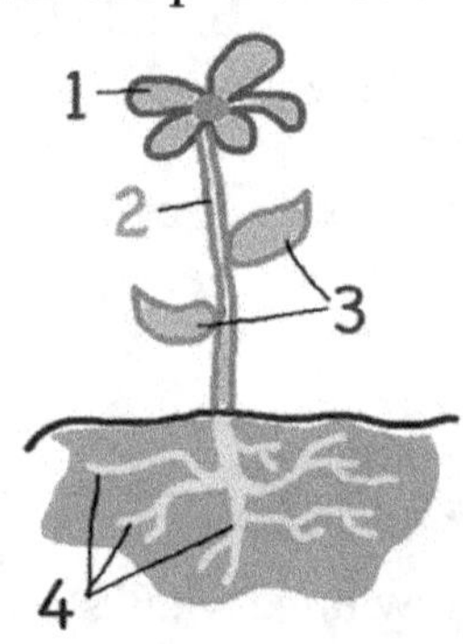

	I	II	III	IV
(A)	3	2	4	1
(B)	3	2	1	4
(C)	2	3	1	4
(D)	1	3	2	4

28. The given pictures show different stages of growth of a plant. Arrange these stages in the correct order.

i. 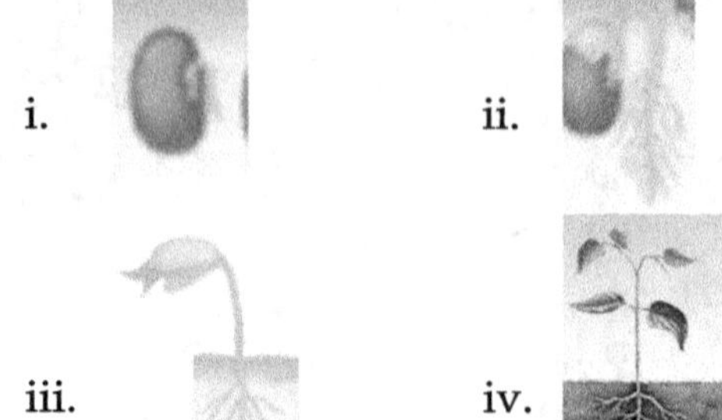   ii.

iii.   iv.

v. 

(A) i, ii, iii, iv, v
(B) iv, v, iii, ii, i
(C) iii, ii, iv, v, i
(D) i, iii, ii, iv, v

29. The given food items can be categorized in three groups. They are ___________.
1. Food of (I) group.
2. Foods of (II) group.
3. Foods of (III) group.

I. 

II.

III.  

Select the correct option.

	I	II	III
(A)	Cereals	Pulses	Vegetables
(B)	Cereals	Pulses	Green leafy vegetables
(C)	Pulses	Vegetables	Tubers and roots
(D)	Cereals	Pulses	Roots and tubers

30. Match column (I) with column (II).

	Column I		Column II
A.	Roots	1.	Supports the plant.
B.	Stem	2.	Reproductive part of plant.
C.	Leaves	3.	Absorb water from soil.
D.	Flowers	4.	Food problem

(A) A-1   B-2   C-3   D-4
(B) A-2   B-3   C-4   D-1
(C) A-3   B-1   C-4   D-2
(D) A-2   B-1   C-3   D-4

Darken Your Choice with HB Pencil

1.	Ⓐ Ⓑ Ⓒ Ⓓ	7.	Ⓐ Ⓑ Ⓒ Ⓓ	13.	Ⓐ Ⓑ Ⓒ Ⓓ	19	Ⓐ Ⓑ Ⓒ Ⓓ	25.	Ⓐ Ⓑ Ⓒ Ⓓ
2.	Ⓐ Ⓑ Ⓒ Ⓓ	8.	Ⓐ Ⓑ Ⓒ Ⓓ	14.	Ⓐ Ⓑ Ⓒ Ⓓ	20.	Ⓐ Ⓑ Ⓒ Ⓓ	26.	Ⓐ Ⓑ Ⓒ Ⓓ
3.	Ⓐ Ⓑ Ⓒ Ⓓ	9.	Ⓐ Ⓑ Ⓒ Ⓓ	15.	Ⓐ Ⓑ Ⓒ Ⓓ	21.	Ⓐ Ⓑ Ⓒ Ⓓ	27.	Ⓐ Ⓑ Ⓒ Ⓓ
4.	Ⓐ Ⓑ Ⓒ Ⓓ	10.	Ⓐ Ⓑ Ⓒ Ⓓ	16.	Ⓐ Ⓑ Ⓒ Ⓓ	22.	Ⓐ Ⓑ Ⓒ Ⓓ	28.	Ⓐ Ⓑ Ⓒ Ⓓ
5.	Ⓐ Ⓑ Ⓒ Ⓓ	11.	Ⓐ Ⓑ Ⓒ Ⓓ	17.	Ⓐ Ⓑ Ⓒ Ⓓ	23.	Ⓐ Ⓑ Ⓒ Ⓓ	29.	Ⓐ Ⓑ Ⓒ Ⓓ
6.	Ⓐ Ⓑ Ⓒ Ⓓ	12.	Ⓐ Ⓑ Ⓒ Ⓓ	18.	Ⓐ Ⓑ Ⓒ Ⓓ	24.	Ⓐ Ⓑ Ⓒ Ⓓ	30.	Ⓐ Ⓑ Ⓒ Ⓓ

CHAPTER 3

ANIMALS

LEARNING OBJECTIVES

➤ Types of animals
➤ Animals and their young ones
➤ Useful animals
➤ Animal habitats
➤ Food for animals

MULTIPLE CHOICE QUESTIONS

Direction: Select the correct alternative from the given options.

1. Which of these animals can live both on land and in water?
   (A) Fish   (B) Crocodile
   (C) Sparrow   (D) Tiger

2. Which of these birds cannot fly?
   (A) Parrot   (B) Cuckoo
   (C) Peacock   (D) Ostrich

3. Who am I?
   (i) I have four legs but I crawl on the ground.
   (ii) I can swim in water.
   (iii) I have a shell to hide.
   (A) Turtle
   (B) Hippopotamus
   (C) Crocodile
   (D) Frog

4. Who am I?
   (i) I am a very faithful pet.
   (ii) I guard your house at night.
   (iii) I am an omnivore.
   (A) Cat
   (B) Parrot
   (C) Crow
   (D) Dog

5. Who am I?
   (i) I am a bird.
   (ii) I am green in colour.
   (iii) I have a long tail and a red break.
   (A) Crow   (B) Sparrow
   (C) Parrot   (D) Peacock

6. Which of these birds cannot fly but can run very fast?

(A) 

Peacock

(B) 

Owl

(C) 

Hen

(D) 

Ostritch

7. Who am I?
   (i) I am the baby of an animal.
   (ii) I will look like a frog when I grow up.

(iii) I am an amphibian.

(A) Crocodile   (B) Lizard

(C) Tadpole   (D) Pup

8. Which of these birds can swim and is not found easily?

(A) Duck   (B) Swan

(C) Sparrow   (D) Crow

9. Look at the puzzles below. Find out how many animals are hidden there? What type of animals are they?

Z	O	Q	S	A	X
X	P	N	M	C	Y
T	U	R	T	L	E
P	T	O	E	G	F

K	L	D	Q	P
R	S	O	O	U
V	X	G	Y	T
M	N	N	G	W

G	M	C	T	B	K	E
I	L	Q	H	N	O	S
D	U	P	A	T	J	R
V	P	A	R	R	O	T

(A) 4 animals; bird, amphibian, domestic, aquatic

(B) 3 animals; amphibian, domestic animal and bird

(C) 5 animals; 2 terrestrial, 1 aquatic, and 2 amphibians

(D) 6 animals; 2 terrestrial, 2 aquatic, and 2 amphibians

10. Which among these lives on land and eats grains?

(A) Frog   (B) Crow

(C) Hen   (D) Pigeon

11. Which of the following animals lives in a burrow?

(A)  Rabbit   (B)  Donkey

(C)  Lion   (D)  Cow

12. Which of the following animals lives in a den?

(A)  Rabbit   (B)  Donkey

(C)  Lion   (D)  Cow

13. We do not get useful things from:

(A) Fish   (B) Cow

(C) Cat   (D) Sheep

14. I am a carnivore and I live in water:

(A)  Crocodile   (B)  Heron

(C)  Walrus   (D)  Swan

15. Find the odd one out:

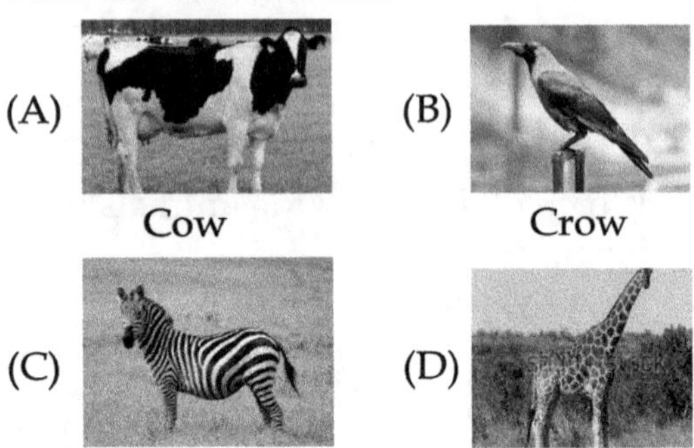

(A) Cow (B) Crow (C) Zebra (D) Giraffe

16. Vultures are __________.
    (A) Aerial herbivores
    (B) Aerial carnivores
    (C) Aerial scavengers
    (D) Arboreal carnivores

17. Circle the wrong set of pictures:
    (A)

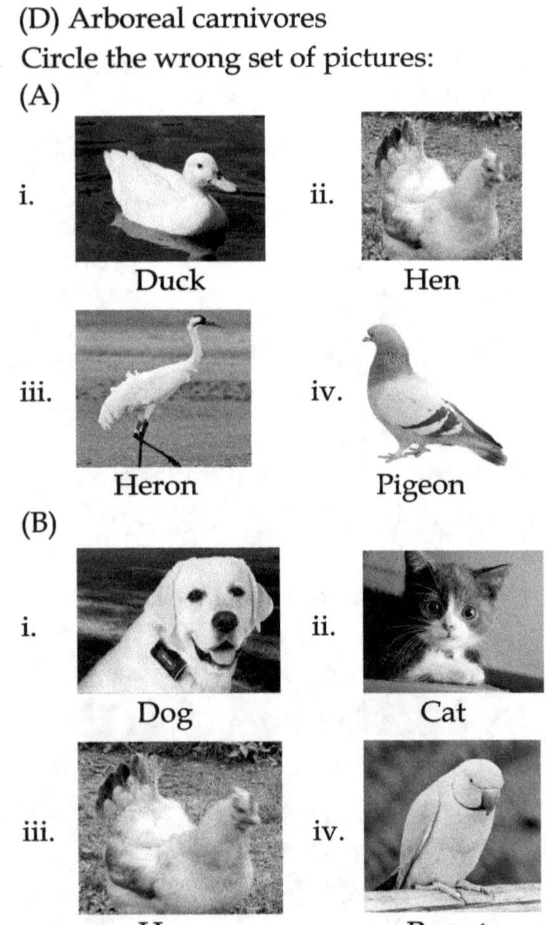

    i. Duck ii. Hen iii. Heron iv. Pigeon
    (B)
    i. Dog ii. Cat iii. Hen iv. Parrot

(C)

i. Elephant ii. Crocodile

iii. Bear iv. Buffalo

(D) None of these

18. Which of these animals has no legs?
    (A) Earthworm
    (B) Butterfly
    (C) Snake
    (D) All of these

19. Which of the following statements is incorrect?
    (A) A giraffe has a very long tongue. It cleans its ear with its tongue.
    (B) Horses and cows sleep while standing up.
    (C) Ants live in anthills or in the bark of trees.
    (D) For a horse, the owner makes a kennel.

20. Which of the following statements is incorrect?
    (A) Cat, goldfish, guinea pig, and parakeet are companions or pet animals.
    (B) Cow, pig, sheep, chicken, and buffalo are not farm animals.
    (C) Animals also make sounds like human beings.
    (D) Animals communicate in many different ways. Some touch, some make noise, and some leave a smell.

21. What sound does the animal in the following image make?

OLYMPIAD WORKBOOK (NSO) CLASS—1

Hen

(A) Bow wow

(B) Meow meow

(C) Cock a doodle doo

(D) Oink oink

22. Which of these animals does not make a sound?

(A) Bee   (B) Sparrow

(C) Duck   (D) Ant

23. Which of these birds make the sound caw caw?

(A) Crow   (B) Parrot

(C) Humming bird   (D) Swan

24. Ducks are ________.

(A) Water animals

(B) Water animals that give eggs

(C) Water animals that give eggs and meat too

(D) Water and land animal that gives both eggs and meat

25. To which of these categories would a parrot belong?

(A) Wild   (B) Pet

(C) Domestic   (D) All of them

HOTS (ACHIEVERS SECTION)

26. The given grid has names of animals hidden in it. How many animals are there?

I. Eat insects.

II. Live in a house made by man.

Q	N	L	P	R	F	G
K	L	I	Z	A	R	D
F	M	O	C	C	O	W
H	E	N	D	O	G	S
X	H	O	R	S	E	B

	I	**II**
(A)	Four	Three
(B)	Three	Four
(C)	Three	Three
(D)	Two	Two

27. Match the following and choose the correct option.

	I	**II**
a.	Frog	i. Roar
b.	Elephant	ii. Croak
c.	Lion	iii. Coo
d.	Pigeon	iv. Moo
		v. Trumpet

(A) a-ii, b-v, c-iv, d-iii

(B) a-ii, b-iii, c-i, d-iv

(C) a-iv, b-v, c-i, d-iii

(D) a-ii, b-v, c-i, d-iii

28. 'X' is the animal and 'Y' is the type of food it eats. Match the following and then choose the correct option.

	X	**Y**
a.	Frog	i. Grains
b.	Eagle	ii. Small insects and grain
c.	Crow	iii. Flesh
d.	Squirrel	iv. Plant parts and insects

(A) a-ii, b-i, c-iii, d-iv

(B) a-i, b-ii, c-iii, d-iv

(C) a-iv, b-iii, c-ii, d-i

(D) a-iii, b-ii, c-iv, d-i

29. The following are the list of animals and foods obtained from them. Match List I with List II.

	List I		List II
A.	Hen	1.	Bird
B.	Cow	2.	Insect
C.	Camel	3.	Lives in desert
D.	Butterfly	4.	Domestic animal

(A) A-2   B-3   C-4   D-1
(B) A-1   B-2   C-4   D-3
(C) A-1   B-4   C-3   D-2
(D) A-2   B-3   C-4   D-1

30. Identify the pair that shows animal and its home correctly.

(A) 

Earthworm   Hole

(B) 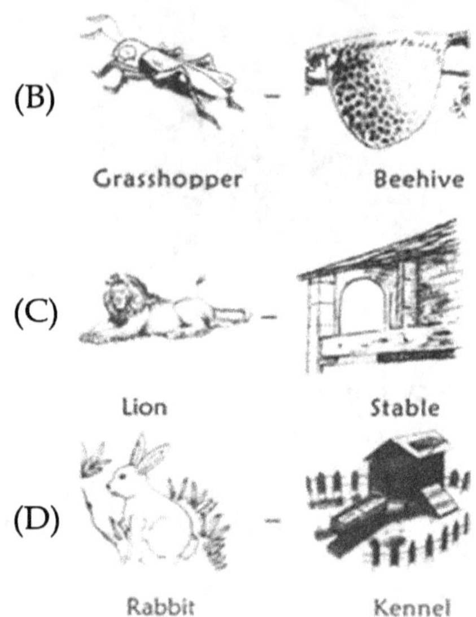

Grasshopper   Beehive

(C)

Lion   Stable

(D)

Rabbit   Kennel

—Darken Your Choice with HB Pencil—

1.	Ⓐ Ⓑ Ⓒ Ⓓ	7.	Ⓐ Ⓑ Ⓒ Ⓓ	13.	Ⓐ Ⓑ Ⓒ Ⓓ	19	Ⓐ Ⓑ Ⓒ Ⓓ	25.	Ⓐ Ⓑ Ⓒ Ⓓ
2.	Ⓐ Ⓑ Ⓒ Ⓓ	8.	Ⓐ Ⓑ Ⓒ Ⓓ	14.	Ⓐ Ⓑ Ⓒ Ⓓ	20.	Ⓐ Ⓑ Ⓒ Ⓓ	26.	Ⓐ Ⓑ Ⓒ Ⓓ
3.	Ⓐ Ⓑ Ⓒ Ⓓ	9.	Ⓐ Ⓑ Ⓒ Ⓓ	15.	Ⓐ Ⓑ Ⓒ Ⓓ	21.	Ⓐ Ⓑ Ⓒ Ⓓ	27.	Ⓐ Ⓑ Ⓒ Ⓓ
4.	Ⓐ Ⓑ Ⓒ Ⓓ	10.	Ⓐ Ⓑ Ⓒ Ⓓ	16.	Ⓐ Ⓑ Ⓒ Ⓓ	22.	Ⓐ Ⓑ Ⓒ Ⓓ	28.	Ⓐ Ⓑ Ⓒ Ⓓ
5.	Ⓐ Ⓑ Ⓒ Ⓓ	11.	Ⓐ Ⓑ Ⓒ Ⓓ	17.	Ⓐ Ⓑ Ⓒ Ⓓ	23.	Ⓐ Ⓑ Ⓒ Ⓓ	29.	Ⓐ Ⓑ Ⓒ Ⓓ
6.	Ⓐ Ⓑ Ⓒ Ⓓ	12.	Ⓐ Ⓑ Ⓒ Ⓓ	18.	Ⓐ Ⓑ Ⓒ Ⓓ	24.	Ⓐ Ⓑ Ⓒ Ⓓ	30.	Ⓐ Ⓑ Ⓒ Ⓓ

HUMAN BEINGS AND THEIR NEEDS

4

➤ Our sense organs
➤ Good habits
➤ Clothes

➤ Balanced food
➤ Shelter

MULTIPLE CHOICE QUESTIONS

Direction: Select the correct alternative from the given options.

1. We have ________ sense organs situated above our________:
   (A) 2, neck
   (B) 3, legs
   (C) 4, stomach
   (D) 5, neck

2. While playing a video game, how many sense organs do we use?
   (A) 2, eyes and ears
   (B) 3, eyes, ears, and skin
   (C) 1, only eyes
   (D) 2, eyes and skin

3. Look at the following picture. The girl in the picture is not well. Can you guess the name of the disease? Also name the two sense organs which are involved in this disease?

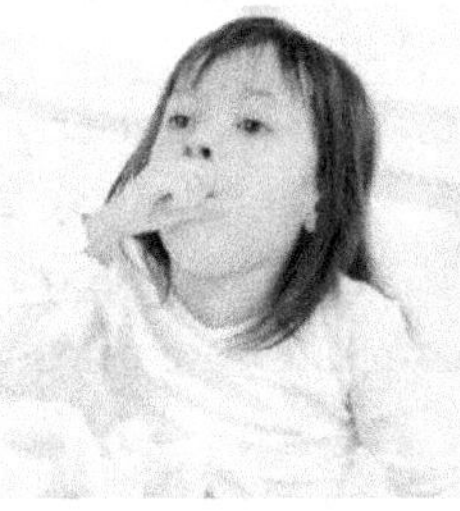

   (A) Cold, Eyes and nose
   (B) Fever, Eyes and ears
   (C) Headache, Tongue and ears
   (D) Cough, Ears and nose

4. Read the poem carefully and find out which sense organ is involved in this activity:

   Jonny Botter bought some butter
   "But", he said, "this butter's bitter"
   So Jonny bought some better butter,
   To make the bitter butter better.
   (A) Mouth
   (B) Nose
   (C) Eyes
   (D) Tongue

5. One evening, when Ananya was studying, she told her mother that she was unable to study since the past few days. Whenever she would try to concentrate, her eyes start hurting.

   Which of her mother's following statement is/are correct?

   i. Ananya, it might be because your eyesight is getting weak, so you should not watch too much television.

   ii. Ananya, it might be because your eye sight is getting weak, so you should have a proper diet.

   iii. Ananya, you can stop studying for a few days.

iv. Ananya, go and wash your eyes properly. It might be because you are not sleeping properly.
(A) Only i   (B) Both i and ii
(C) i, ii, and iii   (D) i, ii, and iv

6. Nutritious food does not give us ________.
(A) Good health   (B) Sickness
(C) Energy to run   (D) Proper growth

7. Amar carries a bag with his ________.
(A) Teeth   (B) Hands
(C) Legs   (D) Nose

8. We use legs for ________.
(A) Holding things   (B) Writing
(C) Drawing   (D) Running

9. Which of these can we smell?
(A) Rose   (B) Perfume
(C) Incense sticks   (D) All of these

10. When do we brush our teeth?
(A) After waking up
(B) After coming from school
(C) After playing
(D) While taking a bath

11. It is important to start the day with nutritious food because ________.
(Which statement is incorrect)
(A) It is the first food of the day.
(B) We haven't eaten anything since night (8–10 hours gap).
(C) It gives us energy for school.
(D) We won't be hungry later on if we start the day with healthy food.

12. Too much of which of these will harm you?
(A) Fruits   (B) Sugar
(C) Cereals   (D) Vegetables

13. An omnivore can eat ________.
(A) Milk   (B) Fruits
(C) Fish   (D) All of these

14. Which of these statements about milk is/are correct?
i.   It is white in colour.
ii. It keeps our bones and teeth healthy.
iii. We should drink milk once a week.
iv. It is a complete food.
(A) i and ii   (B) i, iii, and iv
(C) i, ii, and iv   (D) Only i

15. We wash utensils in this room. What is this room called?
(A) Guest room   (B) Kitchen
(C) Drawing room   (D) Bedroom

16. Strike out the picture showing the wrong practice:

i.   ii.

iii.   iv.

(A) i   (B) ii
(C) i and ii   (D) All of these

17. See the following table.

S.No	Thing	We must do	We must not do
1.	Eat lots of sweets		✓
2.	Eat healthy food	✓	
3.	Drink cold drinks	✓	
4.	Brush my teeth		✓
5.	Sleep late		✓

How many 'ticks' are correct there?
(A) 3   (B) 2
(C) 5   (D) All are wrong

18. When we sneeze, we must say ________.
(A) Please.
(B) Excuse me!
(C) Thank you!
(D) Congratulations!

OLYMPIAD WORKBOOK (NSO) CLASS–1

19. In which of the following rooms of our house, do we attend to our guests?
    (A) Bedroom   (B) Bathroom
    (C) Drawing room   (D) Kitchen

20. We get wool from _________.
    (A) Animals
    (B) Plants
    (C) Chemical reactions
    (D) Jungles

21. Complete the following sentences by choosing the correct sequence of words.
    i.   We wear _________ to protect our body.
    ii. We need a _________ to live in.
    iii. _________ helps us to grow and stay healthy.
    (A) Milk; food; clothes
    (B) Sheep; bathroom; clothes
    (C) Clothes; house; food
    (D) Milk; food; clothes

22. We wear these clothes in winter _________.
    (A) Cotton clothes
    (B) Woollen clothes
    (C) Rain coat
    (D) All of them

23. Our handkerchief:
    (A) In winters, it should be made of wool.
    (B) In summers, it should be made of cotton.
    (C) It should be made up of cotton only.
    (D) In rainy season, it should be made of synthetic fibre.

24. Rain coats and umbrellas are made up of _________.
    (A) Plastic   (B) Rubber
    (C) Cotton   (D) Wool

25. Sarees can be made of _________.
    (A) Cotton fibres
    (B) Woolen fibres
    (C) Synthetic fibres
    (D) Both (A) and (C)

HOTS (ACHIEVERS SECTION)

26. Read the following questions. Which option suits I and II?
    I. Which part of our body moves outwards and inwards during breathing?
    II. Which part of our body moves the most during cycling?

	I	II
(A)	Lungs	Heart
(B)	Lungs	Legs
(C)	Nose	Hands
(D)	Nose	Mouth

27. Which of the following words is correctly associated with the given sense organs?

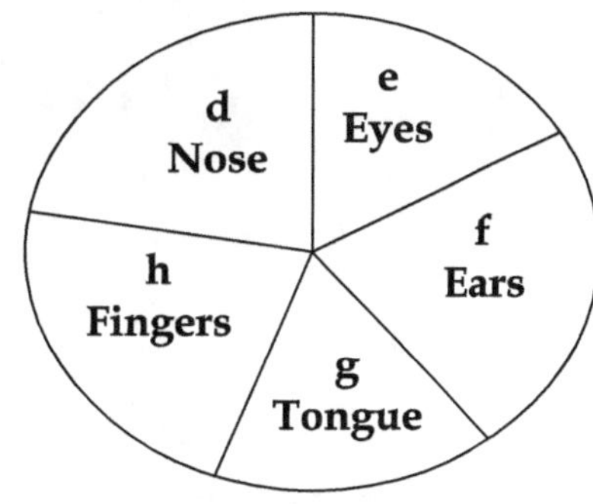

    (A) d-Fragrance, e-Sweet
    (B) g-Delicious, e-Sound
    (C) h-Touch, d-Fragrance
    (D) f-Observe, g-Listen

28. The given picture shows a house with four rooms P, Q, R, and S. Where would you most likely to do the following activities?

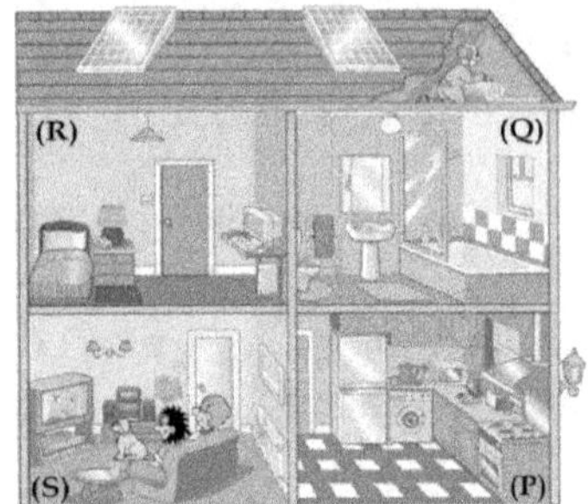

I.   Wash clothes and bathe
II. Cook food
III. Rest and sleep

	I	II	III
(A)	P	Q	S
(B)	Q	P	R
(C)	P	Q	R
(D)	S	P	Q

29. What does the given picture show?

(A) Humans need food.
(B) Humans breathe in air.
(C) Humans grow up.
(D) Humans need clothes.

30. ______ is a sense organ that is NOT needed in the given activity.

(A) Eye   (B) Ear
(C) Nose   (D) None of these

1.	Ⓐ Ⓑ Ⓒ Ⓓ	7.	Ⓐ Ⓑ Ⓒ Ⓓ	13.	Ⓐ Ⓑ Ⓒ Ⓓ	19	Ⓐ Ⓑ Ⓒ Ⓓ	25.	Ⓐ Ⓑ Ⓒ Ⓓ
2.	Ⓐ Ⓑ Ⓒ Ⓓ	8.	Ⓐ Ⓑ Ⓒ Ⓓ	14.	Ⓐ Ⓑ Ⓒ Ⓓ	20.	Ⓐ Ⓑ Ⓒ Ⓓ	26.	Ⓐ Ⓑ Ⓒ Ⓓ
3.	Ⓐ Ⓑ Ⓒ Ⓓ	9.	Ⓐ Ⓑ Ⓒ Ⓓ	15.	Ⓐ Ⓑ Ⓒ Ⓓ	21.	Ⓐ Ⓑ Ⓒ Ⓓ	27.	Ⓐ Ⓑ Ⓒ Ⓓ
4.	Ⓐ Ⓑ Ⓒ Ⓓ	10.	Ⓐ Ⓑ Ⓒ Ⓓ	16.	Ⓐ Ⓑ Ⓒ Ⓓ	22.	Ⓐ Ⓑ Ⓒ Ⓓ	28.	Ⓐ Ⓑ Ⓒ Ⓓ
5.	Ⓐ Ⓑ Ⓒ Ⓓ	11.	Ⓐ Ⓑ Ⓒ Ⓓ	17.	Ⓐ Ⓑ Ⓒ Ⓓ	23.	Ⓐ Ⓑ Ⓒ Ⓓ	29.	Ⓐ Ⓑ Ⓒ Ⓓ
6.	Ⓐ Ⓑ Ⓒ Ⓓ	12.	Ⓐ Ⓑ Ⓒ Ⓓ	18.	Ⓐ Ⓑ Ⓒ Ⓓ	24.	Ⓐ Ⓑ Ⓒ Ⓓ	30.	Ⓐ Ⓑ Ⓒ Ⓓ

GOOD HABITS AND SAFETY RULES

MULTIPLE CHOICE QUESTIONS

Direction: Select the correct alternative from the given options.

1. At home we should play with _______.
   (A) Electrical gadgets
   (B) Battery-operated toys
   (C) Electric switches
   (D) Utensils

2. When we are crossing the road, we should _______.
   (A) Use a zebra crossing
   (B) Cross from anywhere on the road
   (C) Raise hands to stop vehicles
   (D) Cross when the 'Walk' sign is red

3. We should feed animals at the zoo with _______.
   (A) Peanuts   (B) Banana
   (C) Gram
   (D) We should not feed animals in the zoo

4. Which of the following is/are correct statements?
   i.   Anil should inform his teacher when his friend Ali gets hurt in the playground.
   ii. Abhas crossed the road at the zebra crossing.
   iii. Mr. Deepak did not stop his car at the red light.
   iv. Teacher says, "Do not push each other. Stand in a queue."
   v.   We should help old people to cross the road.
   (A) i and ii   (B) i, ii, and iii
   (C) i, ii, iv, and v (D) All of these

5. When do kids need to wear a life jacket?
   (A) When on a boat
   (B) When near an open body of water
   (C) When playing a water sport
   (D) All of these

6. Look at the following pictures carefully. What is the picture showing?

   (A) Zebra crossing
   (B) Pedestrian crossing
   (C) Both (A) and (B)
   (D) No speed limit zone

7. Which of the following should not be touched with wet hands?
   (A) Toys
   (B) Electrical switches
   (C) Electric appliance
   (D) Both (B) and (C)

8. We should not fly kites _______.
   (A) On the open terrace
   (B) In open grounds
   (C) In school ground
   (D) In parks

9. Playing at the playground is a lot of fun if you play safely. How can you keep the playground safe?
   (A) Do not jump off the swings.
   (B) Make sure an adult you trust is watching you.
   (C) Do not push, shove, or play rough.
   (D) All of these

10. Choose the correct match:

Column A	Column B
1. Crossing Road	(i) Books and toys
2. Zoo	(ii) Toys
3. Organic	(iii) Zebra crossing
4. Play with	(iv) Maintain distance

   (A) 1-iii, 2-ii, 3-i, 4-iv
   (B) 1-ii, 2-iv, 3-i, 4-iii
   (C) 1-iii, 2-iv, 3-i, 4-ii
   (D) 1-iii, 2-i, 3-iv, 4-ii

11. Choose the correct sequence in the following sentence.
    Obey the traffic rules. __________ when the light is red and __________ when it is green.
    (A) Go, stop
    (B) Stop, go
    (C) Wait, go
    (D) Stop, wait

12. We should use __________, __________, or __________ while swimming.
    (A) Tubes, clothes, arm bands
    (B) Floaters, tubes, arm bands
    (C) Floaters, swimming appliances, arm bands
    (D) Floaters, tubes, arm sequences

13. How can you put the given things in a group?

    (A) Things that can burn our fingers
    (B) Things that can hurt us
    (C) Things that can cut our hand
    (D) Things with sharp edges

14. Jaya was throwing things here and there in the room. Her mother told her, don't do this, this will _______.
    (A) Help us to clean the house
    (B) Help her to find things easily
    (C) Make her or someone else trip on things
    (D) Make her dirty

15. On road always walk _______.
    (A) Anywhere you want
    (B) On your right side
    (C) On your left side
    (D) In the centre

16. Who am I?
    i. You must walk on me when you cross the road.
    ii. I have two colours.
    (A) Traffic crossing
    (B) Horse crossing
    (C) Footpath
    (D) Zebra crossing

17. Do you follow safety rules? Which are the incorrect activities?
    i. I throw banana peels and other wrappers on the road.
    ii. I play with matchsticks at home.
    iii. I run up and down the stairs in school.
    iv. I get down from the moving school bus.
    (A) i and ii
    (B) i, ii, and iii
    (C) i and iv
    (D) All of these

18. Complete the following sentence:

    We should make a __________ while getting on a bus.
    (A) Circle
    (B) Queue
    (C) Horizontal line
    (D) Triangle

19. Who am I?

    I am used by people to walk alongside the road.
    (A) Zebra crossing
    (B) Rail crossing
    (C) Footpath
    (D) Rail path

20. Cautionary traffic sign is of what shape?
    (A) Circular
    (B) Square
    (C) Triangular
    (D) Rectangular

HOTS (ACHIEVERS SECTION)

21. The given items can be categorized into which of the following two groups?

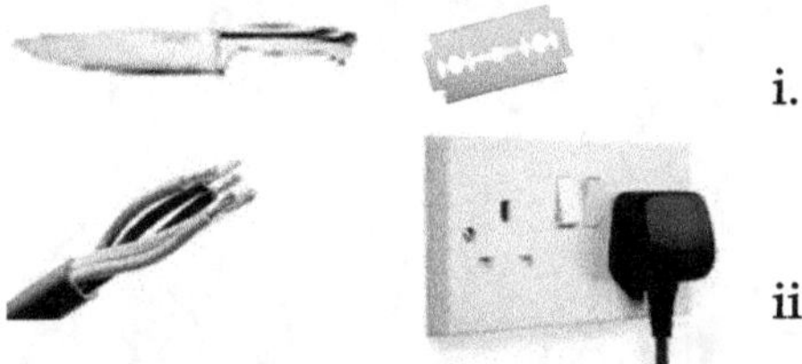

    i. Things that can (I)
    ii. Things that can (II)
    Select the correct option.

	I	II
(A)	Cut	Infect
(B)	Cut	Give electric shock
(C)	Burn	Cut
(D)	Burn	Infect

22. Amit's mother gave him a banana to eat. He ate it on the way to his school. What should he do with the banana peel?
    (A) He should throw it on the road.
    (B) He should throw it in the nearby garden.
    (C) He should keep it in his friend's bag.
    (D) He should throw it in the dustbin.

23. Consider the following statement and choose the correct option

    Statement A: We should take bath twice

    Statement B: We should cross the road using footpath.
    (A) Statement A is true, statement B is false.
    (B) Statement A is false, statement B is true.
    (C) Both the statement are true.
    (D) Both the statement are false.

24. Match the column I and column II

Column I		Column II	
A.	Burning	1.	Zebra crossing
B.	Cut	2.	Rub ice on the affected area
C.	Traffic rules	3.	Make the person lie down
D.	Faint	4.	Apply antiseptic lotion after washing

(A) A-3, B-1, C-2, D-4
(B) A-2, B-4, C-1, D-3
(C) A-1, B-2, C-3, D-4
(D) A-2, B-1, C-3, D-4

25. Read the following sentences carefully and write True/False (T/F)
   A. We should run on a wet floor.
   B. Toys should not be scattered on the floor.
   C. Always cross the road using zebra crossing.

(A) TTF   (B) FTT
(C) TFT   (D) TTT

1.	Ⓐ Ⓑ Ⓒ Ⓓ	6.	Ⓐ Ⓑ Ⓒ Ⓓ	11.	Ⓐ Ⓑ Ⓒ Ⓓ	16	Ⓐ Ⓑ Ⓒ Ⓓ	21.	Ⓐ Ⓑ Ⓒ Ⓓ
2.	Ⓐ Ⓑ Ⓒ Ⓓ	7.	Ⓐ Ⓑ Ⓒ Ⓓ	12.	Ⓐ Ⓑ Ⓒ Ⓓ	17.	Ⓐ Ⓑ Ⓒ Ⓓ	22.	Ⓐ Ⓑ Ⓒ Ⓓ
3.	Ⓐ Ⓑ Ⓒ Ⓓ	8.	Ⓐ Ⓑ Ⓒ Ⓓ	13.	Ⓐ Ⓑ Ⓒ Ⓓ	18.	Ⓐ Ⓑ Ⓒ Ⓓ	23.	Ⓐ Ⓑ Ⓒ Ⓓ
4.	Ⓐ Ⓑ Ⓒ Ⓓ	9.	Ⓐ Ⓑ Ⓒ Ⓓ	14.	Ⓐ Ⓑ Ⓒ Ⓓ	19.	Ⓐ Ⓑ Ⓒ Ⓓ	24.	Ⓐ Ⓑ Ⓒ Ⓓ
5.	Ⓐ Ⓑ Ⓒ Ⓓ	10.	Ⓐ Ⓑ Ⓒ Ⓓ	15.	Ⓐ Ⓑ Ⓒ Ⓓ	20.	Ⓐ Ⓑ Ⓒ Ⓓ	25.	Ⓐ Ⓑ Ⓒ Ⓓ

AIR AND WATER

6

LEARNING OBJECTIVES

➤ Properties of air
➤ Uses of water
➤ Sources of water

MULTIPLE CHOICE QUESTIONS

Direction: Select the correct alternative from the given options.

1. Which of the following moves with the help of air?
   (A) Bat
   (B) Boat
   (C) Boy
   (D) Dog

2. Which of the following does not breathe in air?
   (A) Parrot
   (B) Rose plant
   (C) Cat
   (D) Toy

3. We need _______ to move a windmill, a boat, and a kite.
   (A) Water
   (B) Air
   (C) Engine
   (D) Storm

4. The given figure shows that _______.

   (A) Air has no weight
   (B) Air occupies space
   (C) Air has volume
   (D) Air is needed for burning

5. Look at the following picture carefully.

   In the above pictures, the girl observed bubbles coming out of the glass when she pushed the glass into the water tub.
   What does this activity show?
   (A) Air has weight
   (B) The empty glass is filled with air
   (C) Air comes out of the water in the form of bubbles
   (D) Water displaces air in the glass

6. The gas in air that supports life is _______.
   (A) Carbon dioxide
   (B) Oxygen
   (C) Nitrogen
   (D) Freon

7. Which option is/are correct?
   i. Air is not present inside a room.
   ii. All living beings need water.
   iii. Water is precious.
   iv. We do not need air to fly a kite.
   (A) i and iv   (B) iii and iv
   (C) ii and iii   (D) i and ii

8. List two examples of each of them.
   Choose the correct sequence:
   i. Natural source of water:
   ii. Water resources on the surface of the Earth:
   iii. Breathing organs:
   iv. Things moving with the help of water:
   (A) River, pond; rivers and lake; nose and lungs; boat, ship
   (B) Nose and lungs; boat, ship; nose and lungs; boat, ship
   (C) Boat, ship; nose and lungs; nose and lungs; boat, ship
   (D) Rivers and lake; nose and lungs; boat, ship; river, pond

9. Some rain water seeps into the ground. This water is called __________.
   (A) Ground water   (B) Surface water
   (C) River water   (D) Pond water

10. When we burn __________ (I), air gets __________ (II). Select correct I and II for the blanks.

I	II
(A) Grass	Dirty
(B) Crackers	Dirty
(C) Paper	Dirty
(D) Paper, grass and crackers	Dirty

11.

Look at the picture. It is showing a __________.
(A) Breezy evening
(B) Stormy evening
(C) Polluted city
(D) wind

12.

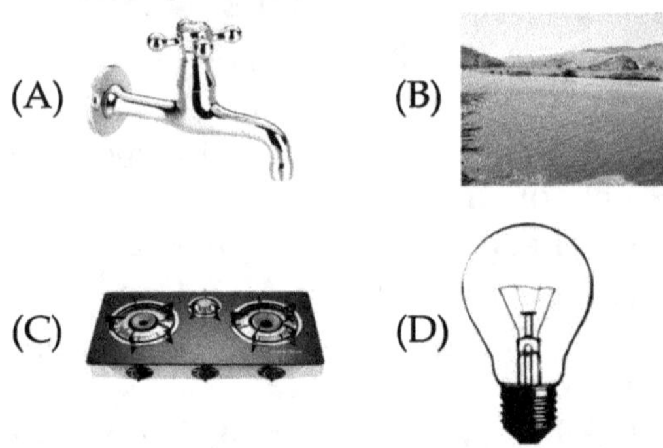

The given picture is perfectly related to the __________.

(A)   (B)

(C)   (D)

13. Which activity we should not perform if we want to save water?
   (A) Use shower for bathing
   (B) Use bucket to wash car
   (C) Turn off the tap while brushing your teeth
   (D) Brush your teeth every day

14. Some rain water seeps into the __________. This water is called __________.
   (A) Ground, ground water
   (B) Ground, surface water
   (C) River, ground water
   (D) River, surface water

15. Choose the correct sequence.
   When we _______ water, the _______ die. Then it becomes _________ for us to drink.

(A) Cool, germs, unsafe
(B) Unsafe, boil, safe
(C) Boil, germs, safe
(D) Boil, germs, unsafe

16. To light a candle, we need __________.
(A) Matchbox   (B) Candle
(C) Air   (D) All of these

17. Which of the following actions show that animals need water?

(A) 

(B)

(C)

(D)

18. __________ is necessary for plants to grow well.
(A) Air   (B) Water
(C) Sunlight   (D) All of these

19. _______ water harvesting is important as it _______ water.
(A) River, save   (B) Sea, save
(C) Rain, save   (D) Ground, save

20.

Look at the pictures carefully. Which of the following helps them to work properly?
(A) Rain   (B) Clouds
(C) Water   (D) Air

21. Select the correct option and solve this puzzle, across.

I.	W		S		E
II.	T		N		S
III.	R		V		R

	I	II	III
(A)	Water	Tank	River
(B)	Waste	Tanks	River
(C)	Water	Tents	River
(D)	Wash	Tanks	Rover

22. Choose the incorrect options.
i. The water in rivers comes from mountains.
ii. All living things need water.
iii. Water is not precious as we can get it easily in homes.
iv. Water is important because we need water to drink.
(A) i and ii   (B) ii and iii
(C) iii   (D) i and iv

23. Fill up the blanks by choosing the correct sequence:
i. Air makes the windmill _______.
ii. Air occupies __________.
iii. All living things need air to _________.
(A) Breathe, space, move
(B) Move, breathe, space
(C) Space, move, breathe
(D) Move, space, breathe

24. When air gets dirty, it is called air _______.
(A) Unsafe   (B) Unusable
(C) Pollution   (D) Disease

25. Very hot winds that blow in summer is called
(A) loo   (B) breeze
(C) storm   (D) wind

26. Look at the given pictures.

I

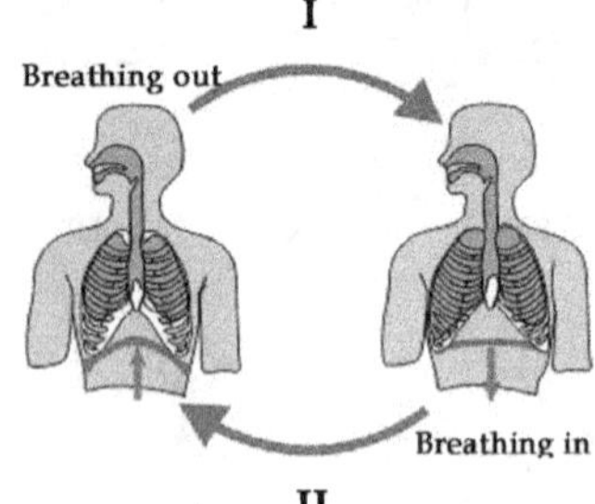

II

Which characteristics of air are highlighted in the pictures?

	I	II
(A)	Air takes up space	Living things breathe air
(B)	Living things breathe air	Air is invisible
(C)	Air is invisible but can be felt	Living things breathe in air through the lungs
(D)	Living things breathe air	Air takes up space

27. Look at the given pictures.

Which characteristic of water is highlighted in the pictures?

(A) Water is tasteless
(B) Water is invisible
(C) Water does not have its own shape
(D) Water is weightless

28. Look at the given picture. Which of the following would be the perfect title for the picture?

(A) Do not waste water.
(B) Conserve water.
(C) Water is precious.
(D) All of these

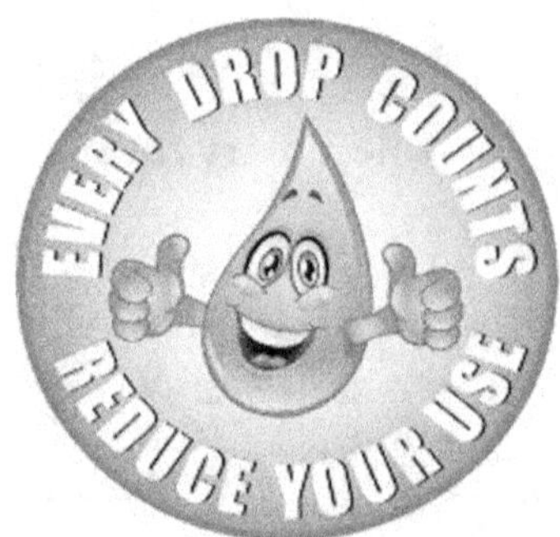

29. This activity performed by the boy in the given picture specifically shows that __________.

(A) Strong wind fills our surroundings.
(B) Moving air is needed to move things.
(C) Moving air has no weight.
(D) All of these

30. Which of the following pictures represent water cycle?

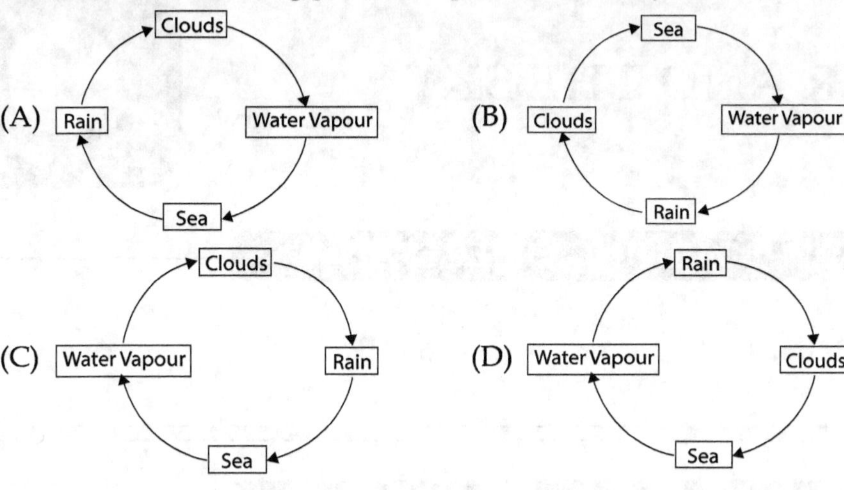

1.	Ⓐ Ⓑ Ⓒ Ⓓ	7.	Ⓐ Ⓑ Ⓒ Ⓓ	13.	Ⓐ Ⓑ Ⓒ Ⓓ	19	Ⓐ Ⓑ Ⓒ Ⓓ	25.	Ⓐ Ⓑ Ⓒ Ⓓ
2.	Ⓐ Ⓑ Ⓒ Ⓓ	8.	Ⓐ Ⓑ Ⓒ Ⓓ	14.	Ⓐ Ⓑ Ⓒ Ⓓ	20.	Ⓐ Ⓑ Ⓒ Ⓓ	26.	Ⓐ Ⓑ Ⓒ Ⓓ
3.	Ⓐ Ⓑ Ⓒ Ⓓ	9.	Ⓐ Ⓑ Ⓒ Ⓓ	15.	Ⓐ Ⓑ Ⓒ Ⓓ	21.	Ⓐ Ⓑ Ⓒ Ⓓ	27.	Ⓐ Ⓑ Ⓒ Ⓓ
4.	Ⓐ Ⓑ Ⓒ Ⓓ	10.	Ⓐ Ⓑ Ⓒ Ⓓ	16.	Ⓐ Ⓑ Ⓒ Ⓓ	22.	Ⓐ Ⓑ Ⓒ Ⓓ	28.	Ⓐ Ⓑ Ⓒ Ⓓ
5.	Ⓐ Ⓑ Ⓒ Ⓓ	11.	Ⓐ Ⓑ Ⓒ Ⓓ	17.	Ⓐ Ⓑ Ⓒ Ⓓ	23.	Ⓐ Ⓑ Ⓒ Ⓓ	29.	Ⓐ Ⓑ Ⓒ Ⓓ
6.	Ⓐ Ⓑ Ⓒ Ⓓ	12.	Ⓐ Ⓑ Ⓒ Ⓓ	18.	Ⓐ Ⓑ Ⓒ Ⓓ	24.	Ⓐ Ⓑ Ⓒ Ⓓ	30.	Ⓐ Ⓑ Ⓒ Ⓓ

7

WEATHER AND THE SKY

LEARNING OBJECTIVES

➤ Universe
➤ Weather

➤ Earth
➤ Seasons

MULTIPLE CHOICE QUESTIONS

Direction: Select the correct alternative from the given options.

1. Most of the Earth's surface has ———.
   (A) Water (B) Land
   (C) Forests (D) Mountains

2. Which of these is a big ball of fire?
   (A) The Sun (B) The Moon
   (C) The Earth (D) The Sky

3. Which of these does not have its own light?
   (A) The Sun (B) The Moon
   (C) The Star (D) Constellations

4. When there is no Moon, it is called _________.
   (A) New Moon
   (B) Full Moon
   (C) Crescent Moon
   (D) Half Moon

5. Match the following columns and choose the correct option:

A	B
i. This planet has air and water	a. Plants
ii. River flows to meet	b. Water
iii. The Earth has three parts of this	c. Mountain
iv. It is very cold here	d. Sea
v. They make their own food	e. Earth

   (A) i-a; ii-b; iii-c; iv-d; v-e
   (B) i-e; ii-d; iii -b; iv-c; v-a
   (C) i-d; ii-a; iii-c; iv-e; v-b
   (D) i-b; ii-c; iii-a; iv-e; v-d

6. Choose the correct option:
   i. Life is present on Earth because of air, water, and land.
   ii. We should protect our Earth by not polluting air, water, and land.
   iii. We should use the 3Rs – REDUCE, RECYCLE, and REUSE.
   (A) i and ii (B) ii only
   (C) i, ii, and iii (D) i and iii

7. When the moon is half, we call it the ———.
   (A) Half Moon (B) No Moon
   (C) A new Moon (D) Full Moon

8. How many stars are present in the sky?
   (A) Three (B) Two
   (C) Many (D) Twenty

9. Who was the first Indian to travel into space?
(A) Kalpana Chawla
(B) Capt. Rakesh Sharma
(C) Sunita Williams
(D) Neil Armstrong

10. Read the following poem carefully.
Little Ronnie likes to play,
Riding on an open horse sleigh
On the moon and with stars
Which shine forever
They look like a world of gems
Wishes to go and touch them.
It's a dream world, Ronnie says
"If I could reach there," he prays.
In the poem, what is the subject?
(A) Stars   (B) Ronnie
(C) Moon   (D) All of these

11. We eat some special food items in different seasons. Name two food items that you eat on the following days:
i.   Very hot day
ii. Rainy day
iii. Very cold day
Choose the correct sequence.
(A) Ice-cream and iced tea; ice tea and pakodas; tea and coffee
(B) Tea and coffee; ice-cream and pakodas; iced tea and ice-cream
(C) Ice-cream and iced tea; tea and pakodas; tea and coffee
(D) Iced tea and pakodas; tea and coffee; ice-cream and iced tea

12. We know that the Earth is a sphere. Earlier, various people in different parts of the world had different opinions about the shape of the Earth.
Find out about them (any three).
(A) Flat, spherical, oblong
(B) Oval, triangle, rectangle
(C) Spherical, flat, rectangle
(D) Oval, oblong, rectangle

13. What is the time duration in between a New Moon and a Full Moon?
(A) One week
(B) Two weeks
(C) Fourteen days
(D) Both (B) and (C)

14. 
The images given suggest which features of the Sun?
(A) The Sun gives us light
(B) The Sun gives us heat which is important for the growth of plants
(C) The Sun is hot
(D) None of these

15. Which of the following shine at night?
(A) Stars and Moon
(B) The Sun
(C) Planets
(D) The Earth

16. Which of the following options are correctly matched?

i. Dull Sun	a.	Cloudy Day
ii. Bright Sun	b.	Summer
iii. Rains	c.	Winter
iv. Snowfall	d.	Sunny Day
v. Strong Breeze	e.	Windy Day

(A) i and iv   (B) i, ii, and v
(C) i and v   (D) iii, iv, and v

17. We use lots of water in which season?
(A) Cold   (B) Winter
(C) Summer   (D) Rainy

18. Which of these is not a standard form of weather?
(A) Summer   (B) Winter
(C) Monsoon   (D) Windy

19. We use sunglasses on a ______.
    (A) Rainy day   (B) Sunny day
    (C) Cloudy day   (D) Cold day
20. Snowfall occurs in ______.
    (A) Plain regions   (B) Deserts
    (C) Seas   (D) Mountains
21. Which of these is not consumed in the winter season?
    (A) Soup
    (B) Watermelon juice
    (C) Wheat porridge
    (D) Hot milk
22. Unscramble the letters to find the items related to weather. Choose the correct sequence.
    1. A I N A O R C T ....
    2. W S A E R T E A ....
    3. S V E L O G ....
    4. N S G S L A S U S E ....
    (A) Raincoat; Sunglasses; Gloves; Sea water
    (B) Sea water; Raincoat; Gloves; Sunglasses
    (C) Raincoat; Sea water; Gloves; Sunglasses
    (D) Sunglasses; Sea water; Raincoat; Gloves

23. What is a scientist who studies weather called?
    (A) Botanist   (B) Climatologist
    (C) Physiologist   (D) Doctor
24. In the following statements, three kids in three different situations are with water, but all the three situations show three different weathers. Choose the correct sequence.
    i.   Kid playing in a swimming pool.
    ii. Kid enjoying with paper boats in puddles.
    iii. Kid in a warm jacket, making a snowman.
    (A) Winter; Rainy; Summer
    (B) Summer; Rainy; Winter
    (C) Rainy; Winter; Summer
    (D) Summer; Winter; Rainy
25. In the months of March and October, the weather is neither hot nor cold. Which season(s) can this be?
    (A) Spring
    (B) Autumn
    (C) Winter
    (D) Both (A) and (B)

HOTS (ACHIEVERS SECTION)

26. Meenu and Shreya were playing games with their doll. Read the following conversation between them.

    Meenu: Shreya, I will ask mommy to stitch a cotton frock for our doll.

    Shreya: Yes Meenu, You are right. Our doll must be feeling ________ wearing woolens in ________.

    Select the correct words and fill the blanks to complete the above conversation.
    (A) Cold; summer
    (B) Hot; summer
    (C) Wet; winter
    (D) Cold; winter
27. Suruchi washed clothes and put it on a clothes line as shown in the picture.

In which of the following conditions would the clothes dry the fastest?

(A) Sunny day

(B) Rainy day

(C) Cold day

(D) Cool, breezy day

28. Direction: Select the correct words and fill in the blanks to complete the conversation.

Read the following conversation between them.

Somya told her mother that her teacher taught the class about different weathers.

Somya: The condition of air surrounding us on any one day is called __________.

Mother: In the months of June to September, there is a lot of rainfall in most places in our country. Which is that season, Somya?

Somya: This is the __________ season. It is also called the __________ season.

(A) Weather; rainy; winter

(B) Weather; winter; monsoon

(C) Season; rainy; monsoon

(D) Weather; rainy; monsoon

29. Match the columns and select the correct option.

Column I	Column II
(A) Summer days are	1. Cold
(B) Winter days are day	2. A windy
(C) A strong wind blows on	3. Rainy
(D) Monsoon days are	4. Hot

(A) a-1, b-2, c-3, d-4

(B) a−4, b-1, c-2, d-3

(C) a-4, b-2, c-1, d-3

(D) a-1, b-4, c-3, d-2

30. Select the correct match of the weather symbol and the item related to that weather.

(A)   - Goggles and Sweater

(B)   - Goggles and Cap

(C)   - Gloves and Cap

(D)   - Umbrella and Cotton Shirt

1.	A B C D	7.	A B C D	13.	A B C D	19	A B C D	25.	A B C D
2.	A B C D	8.	A B C D	14.	A B C D	20.	A B C D	26.	A B C D
3.	A B C D	9.	A B C D	15.	A B C D	21.	A B C D	27.	A B C D
4.	A B C D	10.	A B C D	16.	A B C D	22.	A B C D	28.	A B C D
5.	A B C D	11.	A B C D	17.	A B C D	23.	A B C D	29.	A B C D
6.	A B C D	12.	A B C D	18.	A B C D	24.	A B C D	30.	A B C D

LOGICAL REASONING

8

LEARNING OBJECTIVES

➤ Identification of missing number
➤ Odd one out (classification)
➤ Finding the missing shape by identifying the relationship
➤ The position or rank of an object or a person
➤ Grouping of figures
➤ Embedded figures
➤ Length
➤ Plane Shapes

MULTIPLE CHOICE QUESTIONS

1. Find the missing number in the given number pattern.

   428, 418, 430, ?, 432, 422, 434, ?

   (A) 418, 436   (B) 422, 444
   (C) 420, 446   (D) 420, 424

2. Which of the following replaces the question mark (?) in given number patterns?

   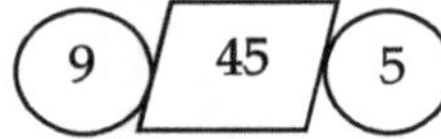

   (A) 43   (B) 42
   (C) 35   (D) 13

3. Complete the number pattern given below.

   4, 12, 36, ?, 324, 972

   (A) 72   (B) 216
   (C) 112   (D) 108

4. Complete the pattern by choosing the next figure.

   (A)    (B)

   (C)    (D)

5. Complete the pattern by choosing the next figure.

   (A)    (B)

   (C)    (D)

6. Find the odd one out.
   (A) Pencil   (B) Clock
   (C) Eraser   (D) Sharpener
7. Find the odd one out.
   (A) Dress   (B) Bat
   (C) Ball   (D) Wicket
8. Find the odd one out.

   (A)    (B) 

   (C)    (D) 

9. Find the odd one out.

   (A)    (B) 

   (C)    (D) 

10. Find the odd one out.

   (A) 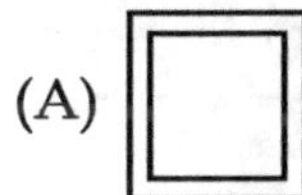   (B) 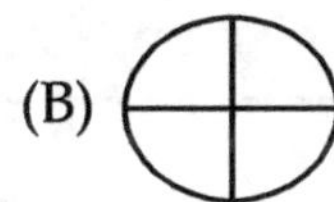

   (C) 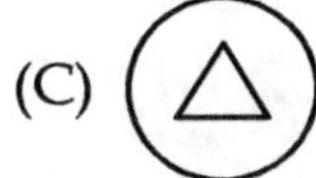   (D) 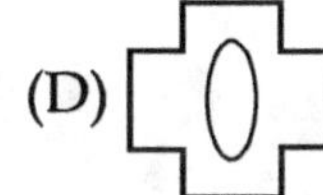

11. Find out the relation.
    Snake : Turtle : : Lizard : ?
    (A) Cat   (B) Fly
    (C) Dog   (D) Crocodile
12. Find the missing shape by identifying the relationship.

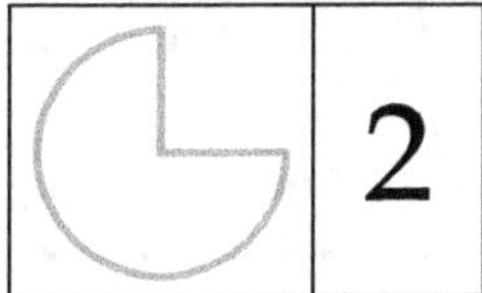 : : 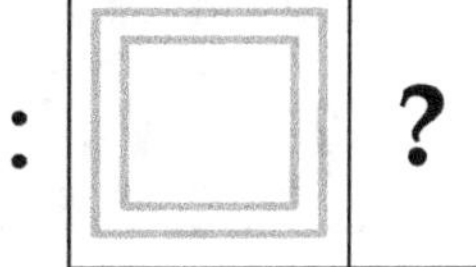

    (A) 8   (B) 4
    (C) 6   (D) 10
13. Find the missing shape by identifying the relationship.

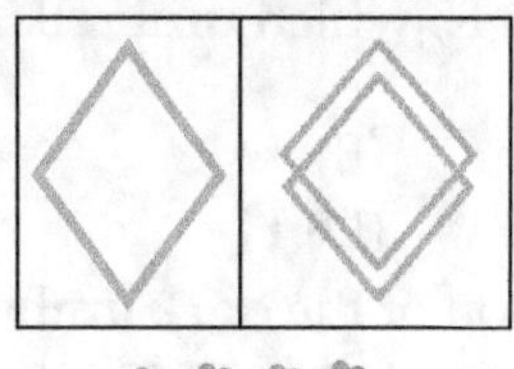 : : 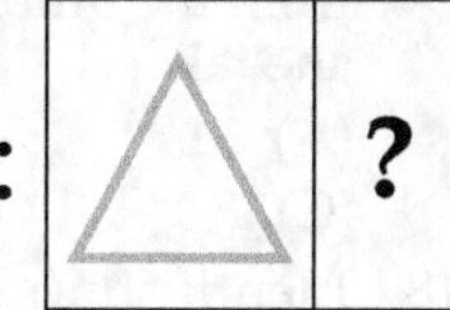

   (A) 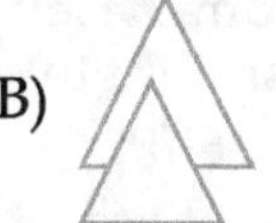   (B) 

14. Find the missing shape by identifying the relationship.

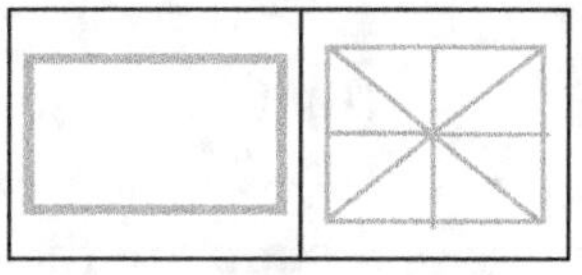 : : 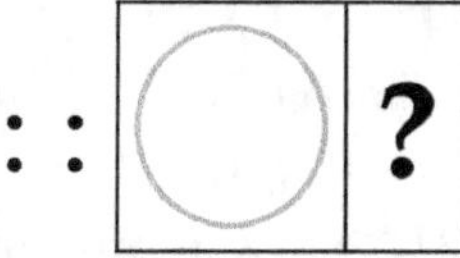

   (A)    (B) 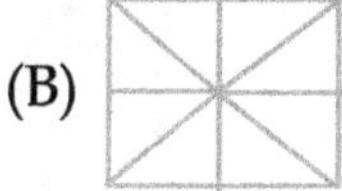

   (C)    (D) 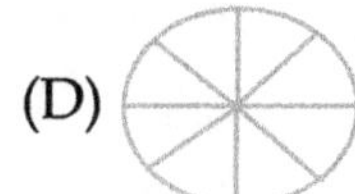

15. Find the missing shape by identifying the relationship.

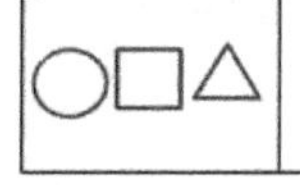 

   (A) 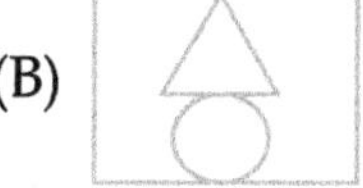   (B)

   (C)    (D)

16. Which umbrella is 10th from the right end?
    (A) D   (B) H
    (C) J   (D) G

17. If Suhani took the immediate left umbrella from the umbrella K, which umbrella did she take?
 (A) M
 (B) N
 (C) F
 (D) H

18. Identify the position of the dark umbrella (from the left) which is just left to red and just right to slanting light umbrella.
 (A) Fifth
 (B) Sixth
 (C) Ninth
 (D) Seventh

19. Umbrella E is _______ to the left of umbrella F.
 (A) Second
 (B) Fourth
 (C) Fifth
 (D) Third

20. Umbrella _______ is the right of F and left of L.
 (A) K
 (B) I
 (C) L
 (D) G

21. How many groups of 3-stars are there?

22. How many groups of 2 rectangles can be formed from the group of assorted shapes given in the box?

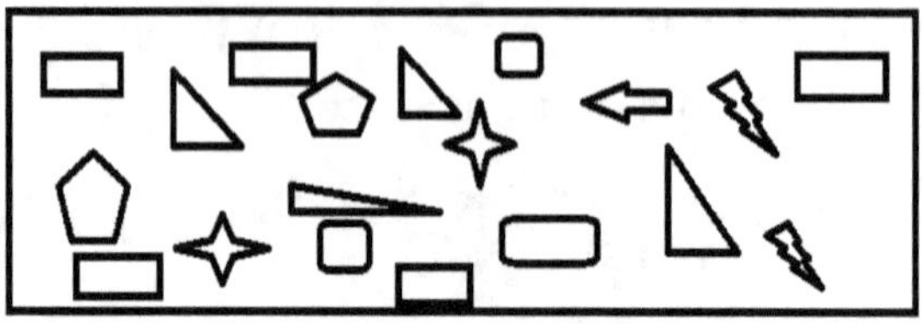

 (A) 1
 (B) 2
 (C) 4
 (D) 3

23. Identify the group in which components can be divided into groups of four equally and completely.

(A)  (B)

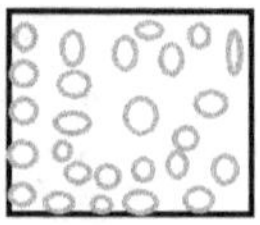

(C)  (D)

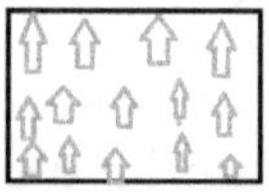

24. How many groups of 2 giraffes are there?

 (A) 10
 (B) 9
 (C) 18
 (D) 20

25. How many groups of 4 bottles are there?

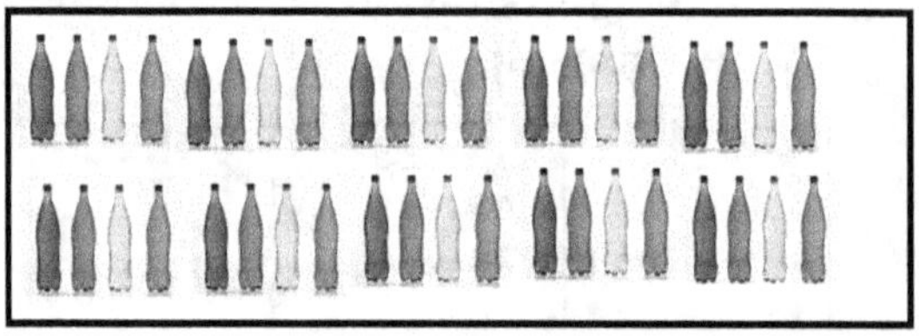

 (A) 10
 (B) 5
 (C) 20
 (C) 40

26. Which of the following is the lightest?

(A) 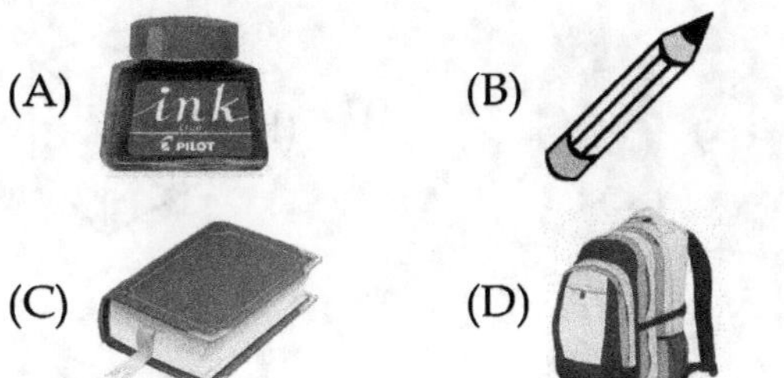
(B)

(C)
(D)

27. Which of the following has the least capacity?

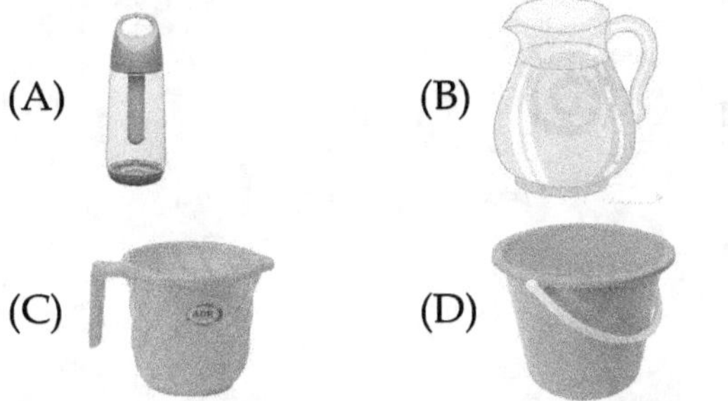

(A)
(B)

(C)
(D)

28. Which of these is lighter than  ?

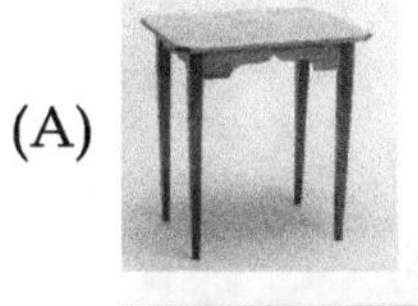

(A)
(B)

(C)
(D) 

29. Which of the two glasses have same height?

(A) Q and S
(B) P and R
(C) P and Q
(D) R and S

30. Spider __________ is the farthest to the ladder.

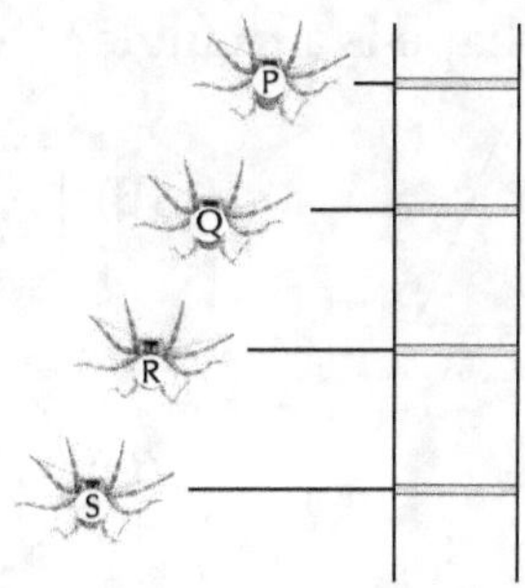

(A) P
(B) Q
(C) R
(D) S

31. Which object can be placed on the chair?

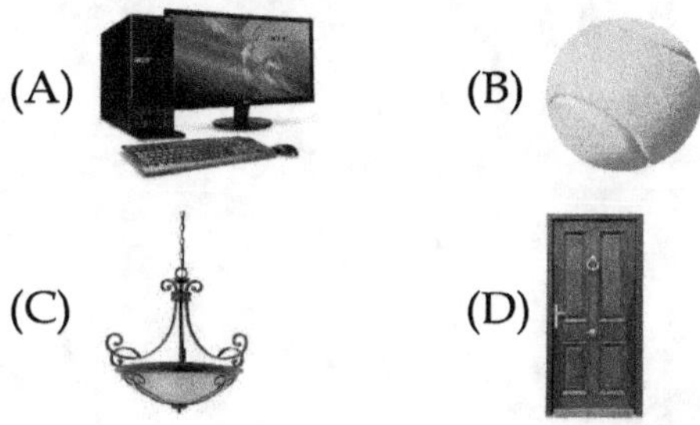

(A)
(B)

(C)
(D)

32. How many circles are there in the figure?

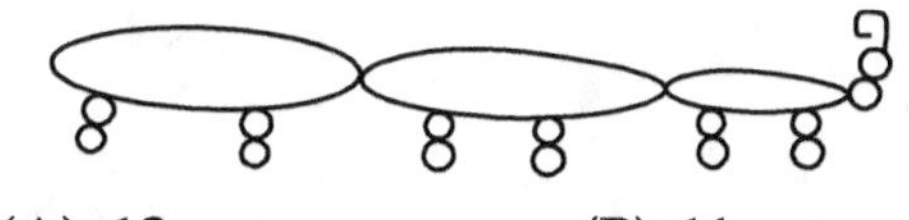

(A) 12
(B) 11
(C) 14
(D) 15

33. Which objects are outside the box?

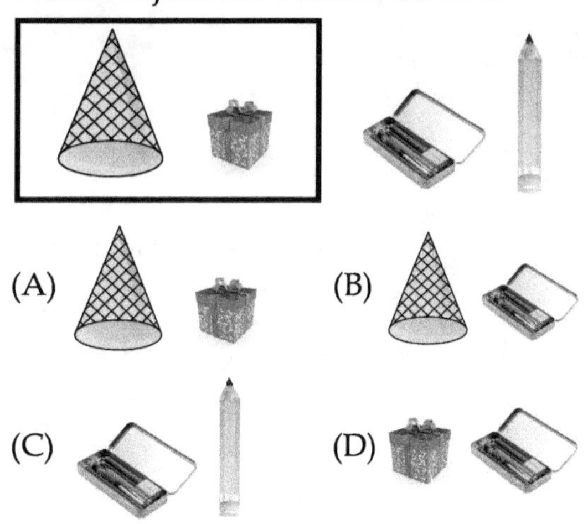

(A)
(B)

(C)
(D)

34. Which shape is a triangle?

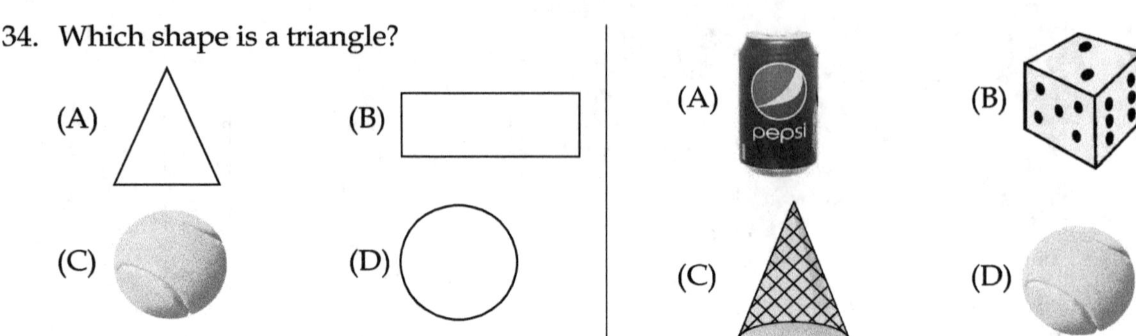

35. Which of the following looks like a cube?

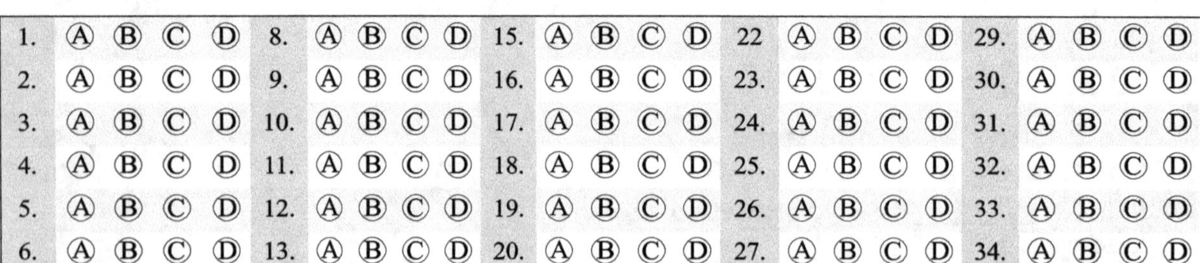

OLYMPIAD WORKBOOK (NSO) CLASS—1

MODEL TEST PAPER

MULTIPLE CHOICE QUESTIONS

1. Which one comes next?

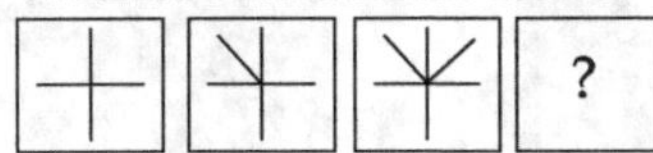

(A) 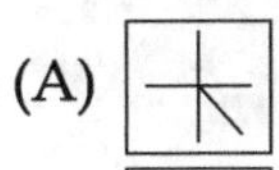 (B) 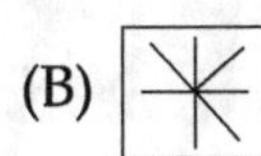

(C) 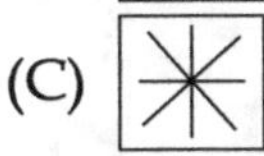 (D) 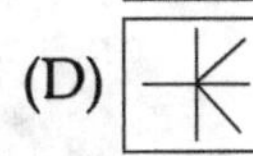

2. What comes next in the given series?

(A) 13   (B) 14
(C) 12   (D) 16

3. What comes next in the given series?

1   11   111   1111   ?

(A) 111   (B) 11111
(C) 1   (D) 11

4. What comes next in the given series?

10   9   8   7   ?

(A) 6   (B) 5
(C) 4   (D) 3

5. What comes next in the given series?

(A) BC   (B) CD
(C) EF   (D) FG

Direction: Select the correct option.

6. Which of the followings is a tree?

(A)    (B)

(C)   (D)

7. Study the following flowchart. Select the correct option to fill empty boxes d, e, and f.

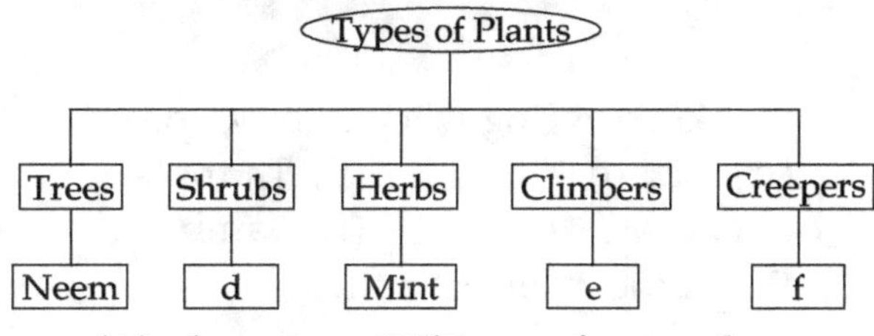

(A) d-grape, e-Hibiscus, f-spinach
(B) d-hibiscus, e-grapevine, f-pumpkin
(C) d-rose, e-pea, f-spinach
(D) d-hibiscus, e-pumpkin, f-rose

8. Which of the following has no seeds in it?

(A) 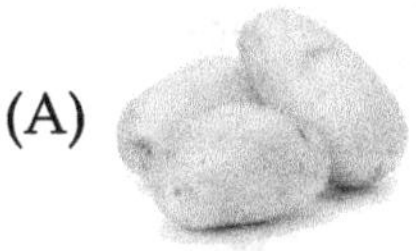   (B) 

(C)    (D) 

9. Match the leaf given below with its fruit:

(A)  (B)

(C) 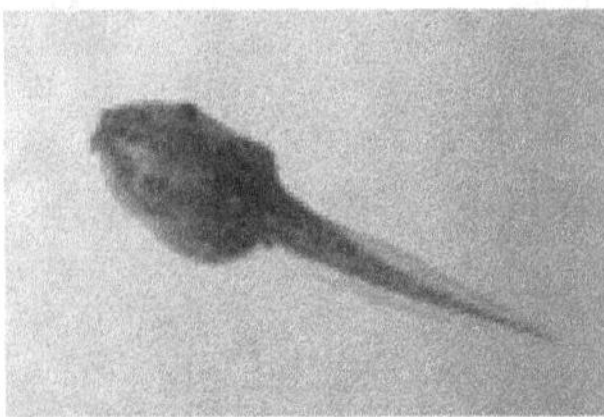 (D)

10. Who am I?

I look like a frog when I grow up.
(A) Lizard   (B) Tadpole
(C) Joey   (D) Lamb

11. Select the incorrect pair.

Animal	Group
(A) Dog	Kennel
(B) Lion	Pride
(C) Elephant	Troop
(D) Ant	Army

12. Which animal/bird lives here?

(A) Duck
(B) Hen
(C) Frog
(D) Both (A) and (C)

13. Which of these animals lives in water and on land?

(A) 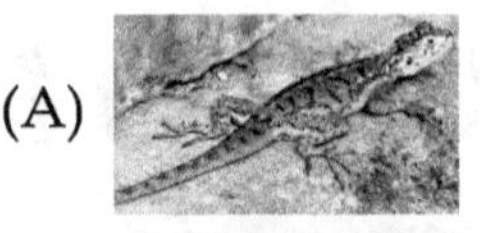   (B) 

(C)    (D) 

14. 

Which sense organ is the child using in the given picture?
(A) Tongue   (B) Nose
(C) Ear   (D) Skin

15. Which of these protects us from the rays of the sun?

(A)    (B) 

(C)    (D) All of these

16. Complete the following sentences by choosing the correct sequence of words:

We need _________________ to cover our body.

We need a _____ to live in.
_______________ helps us to grow and stay healthy.
(A) Shirt, room, *roties*
(B) Clothes, room, food
(C) Clothes, house, food
(D) Plant, house, exercise

17. Which of the following sense organs helps us to know the taste of food?
(A) Skin
(B) Nose
(C) Tongue
(D) Eyes

18. Which of these food products is made of milk?

(A) 
(B) 
(C) 
(D) Both (A) and (B)

19. Which of the following do we eat the most in a day?
(A) Bread
(B) Apple
(C) cheese
(D) Roties

20. Which of the following activities is a bad habit?

(A) 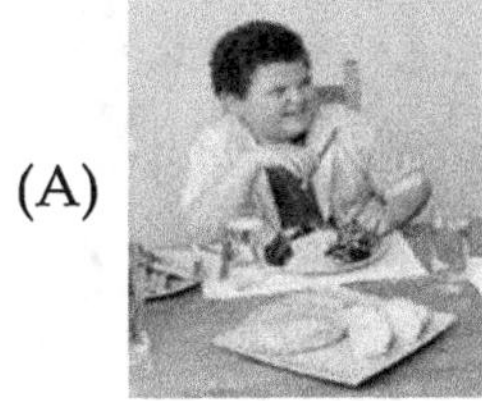
(B) 
(C) 
(D) 

21. Which of the following is correct?

Do's	Don'ts
(A) Cover your ears with ear buds	Comb your hair
(B) Cut nails with a nail cutter	Rinse mouth with water after eating
(C) Bite your nails	Lick your fingers after eating
(D) Clean your ears with ear buds	Bite your nails

22. Soni: I clean my ears with ear buds.
Sanchit: I splash my eyes with water many times a day to freshen my eyes.
Ananya: I use a dirty hanky to blow my nose.
Which child has developed unsafe habit for cleaning the body?
(A) Soni and Sanchit
(B) Sanchit
(C) Ananya
(D) Sanchit and Ananya

23. Which of the following traffic signs indicates a zebra crossing?

(A) 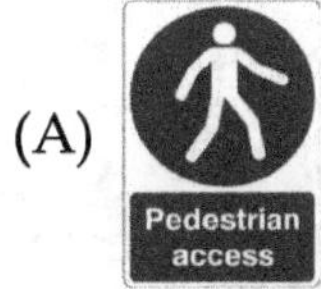

(B) 
(C) 
(D) 

24. Starting from D, cross (X) out every second letter. Which word do you get?
D W T A I T L E K R
(A) Wind
(B) Water
(C) Wink
(D) Wash

25. The given image shows that moving air __________.

(A) has no weight
(B) has weight
(C) cannot dry clothes
(D) can be seen

26. Complete the following paragraph by choosing the correct sequence of words.

We all need __________ to live. Clean water should not be __________.

Plants need water to __________.
Loss of water can cause a plant to __________.

(A) Water, wasted; grow, wilt
(B) Air, thrown; wilt, die
(C) Food, wasted; grow, wilt
(D) Water, wasted; grow, wilt

27. During this/these season(s) weather is neither hot nor cold?

(A) Autumn
(B) Winter
(C) Spring
(D) Both (A) and (C)

28. Unscramble the letters to find the items related to weather.

i.   A I N A O R C T ....
ii. W S A E R T E ....
iii. S V E L O G ....
iv. N S G S L A S U S E ....

(A) Raincoat, Sunglasses, Glove, Sea water
(B) Sea water, Raincoat, Gloves, Sunglasses
(C) Raincoat, Sea water, Gloves, Sunglasses
(D) Sunglasses, Sea water, Raincoat, Gloves

29. A group of stars is called __________.

(A) Constellation
(B) Constanlation
(C) Contentlation
(D) Group

30. Which of the following statements is correct?

(A) The Moon gives us light in the day.
(B) The Moon reflects the light from the Sun that falls on it.
(C) The Sun changes its shape every day.
(D) Stars are very far from us.

31. I. Which portion of the road is shown in the given picture?

II. Which traffic light would the driver in the car have seen before stopping?

	I	II
(A)	Zebra crossing	Red or Yellow
(B)	Middle of the road	Yellow
(C)	Footpath	Green
(D)	Car parking	Red

32. 'X' are the food items obtained from plants and 'Y' are the food items obtained from animals. Choose the correct option.

	X	Y
(A)	Rice, eggs and sugar	Milk, eggs and ghee
(B)	Eggs, ghee and carrot	Rice, milk and sugar
(C)	Ghee and carrot	Rice, milk, sugar and eggs
(D)	Carrot, rice and sugar	Milk, eggs and ghee

33. Some sources of water have been given in the crossword. Solve the crossword and find which of the following words are not present in the crossword?

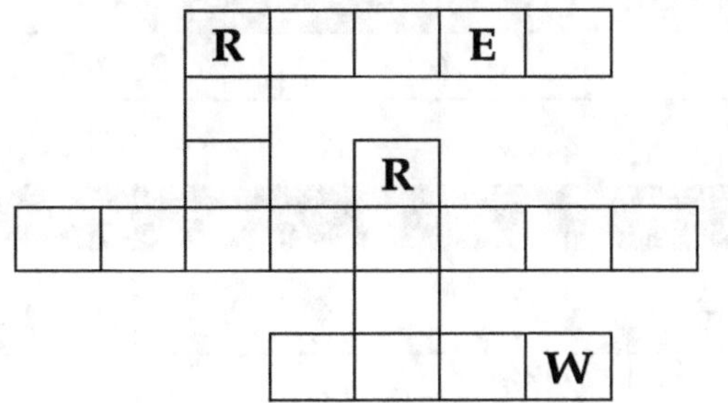

(A) RIVER
(B) SNOW
(C) RAIN
(D) TUBEWELL

34. Starting from leftmost T, cross (×) out every second letter. Whose name did you get?

T K Y A T L S P M A X N C A Z C O H L A P W C L T A

(A) Sania Mirza
(B) Sunita Williams
(C) Kalpana Chawla
(D) Saina Nehwal

35. Which of the following is incorrect?
(A) Go to bed early so that you can wake up early in the morning.
(B) Cover your face when you sleep.
(C) Children need to sleep for eight hours every night.
(D) Our body gets rest when we sleep.

1.	Ⓐ Ⓑ Ⓒ Ⓓ	8.	Ⓐ Ⓑ Ⓒ Ⓓ	15.	Ⓐ Ⓑ Ⓒ Ⓓ	22	Ⓐ Ⓑ Ⓒ Ⓓ	29.	Ⓐ Ⓑ Ⓒ Ⓓ
2.	Ⓐ Ⓑ Ⓒ Ⓓ	9.	Ⓐ Ⓑ Ⓒ Ⓓ	16.	Ⓐ Ⓑ Ⓒ Ⓓ	23.	Ⓐ Ⓑ Ⓒ Ⓓ	30.	Ⓐ Ⓑ Ⓒ Ⓓ
3.	Ⓐ Ⓑ Ⓒ Ⓓ	10.	Ⓐ Ⓑ Ⓒ Ⓓ	17.	Ⓐ Ⓑ Ⓒ Ⓓ	24.	Ⓐ Ⓑ Ⓒ Ⓓ	31.	Ⓐ Ⓑ Ⓒ Ⓓ
4.	Ⓐ Ⓑ Ⓒ Ⓓ	11.	Ⓐ Ⓑ Ⓒ Ⓓ	18.	Ⓐ Ⓑ Ⓒ Ⓓ	25.	Ⓐ Ⓑ Ⓒ Ⓓ	32.	Ⓐ Ⓑ Ⓒ Ⓓ
5.	Ⓐ Ⓑ Ⓒ Ⓓ	12.	Ⓐ Ⓑ Ⓒ Ⓓ	19.	Ⓐ Ⓑ Ⓒ Ⓓ	26.	Ⓐ Ⓑ Ⓒ Ⓓ	33.	Ⓐ Ⓑ Ⓒ Ⓓ
6.	Ⓐ Ⓑ Ⓒ Ⓓ	13.	Ⓐ Ⓑ Ⓒ Ⓓ	20.	Ⓐ Ⓑ Ⓒ Ⓓ	27.	Ⓐ Ⓑ Ⓒ Ⓓ	34.	Ⓐ Ⓑ Ⓒ Ⓓ
7.	Ⓐ Ⓑ Ⓒ Ⓓ	14.	Ⓐ Ⓑ Ⓒ Ⓓ	21.	Ⓐ Ⓑ Ⓒ Ⓓ	28.	Ⓐ Ⓑ Ⓒ Ⓓ	35.	Ⓐ Ⓑ Ⓒ Ⓓ

HINTS AND SOLUTIONS

1. LIVING AND NON-LIVING THINGS

Answer Key

1. (B)	2. (D)	3. (C)	4. (C)	5. (D)	6. (A)	7. (B)	8. (C)	9. (C)	10. (C)
11. (A)	12. (A)	13. (D)	14. (C)	15. (A)					

HOTS (ACHIEVERS SECTION)

16. (c)	17. (b)	18. (b)	19. (c)	20. (c)

2. PLANTS

Answer Key

1. (C)	2. (B)	3. (B)	4. (D)	5. (B)	6. (C)	7. (A)	8. (D)	9. (C)	10. (A)
11. (D)	12. (B)	13. (B)	14. (B)	15. (C)	16. (C)	17. (C)	18. (B)	19. (C)	20. (B)
21. (B)	22. (D)	23. (C)	24. (A)	25. (A)					

HOTS (ACHIEVERS SECTION)

26. (A)	27. (D)	28. (A)	29. (D)	30. (C)

3. ANIMALS

Answer Key

1. (B)	2. (D)	3. (A)	4. (D)	5. (C)	6. (D)	7. (C)	8. (B)	9. (B)	10. (C)
11. (A)	12. (C)	13. (C)	14. (A)	15. (B)	16. (C)	17. (C)	18. (D)	19. (D)	20. (B)
21. (C)	22. (D)	23. (A)	24. (C)	25. (D)					

HOTS (ACHIEVERS SECTION)

26. (C)	27. (D)	28. (C)	29. (C)	30. (A)

4. HUMAN BEINGS ANDD THEIR NEEDS

Answer Key

1. (D)	2. (B)	3. (D)	4. (D)	5. (D)	6. (B)	7. (B)	8. (D)	9. (D)	10. (A)
11. (D)	12. (B)	13. (D)	14. (C)	15. (B)	16. (B)	17. (A)	18. (B)	19. (C)	20. (A)
21. (C)	22. (B)	23. (C)	24. (A)	25. (D)					

HOTS (ACHIEVERS SECTION)

26. (B)	27. (C)	28. (B)	29. (C)	30. (C)

5. FOLLOW SAFETY RULES

Answer Key

1. (b)	2. (a)	3. (d)	4. (c)	5. (d)	6. (c)	7. (d)	8. (a)	9. (d)	10. (c)
11. (b)	12. (b)	13. (b)	14. (c)	15. (c)	16. (d)	17. (d)	18. (b)	19. (c)	20. (c)

HOTS (ACHIEVERS SECTION)

21. (B)	22. (D)	23. (D)	24. (B)	25. (B)

6. AIR AND WATER

Answer Key

1. (B)	2. (D)	3. (B)	4. (B)	5. (B)	6. (B)	7. (C)	8. (A)	9. (A)	10. (D)
11. (B)	12. (A)	13. (A)	14. (A)	15. (C)	16. (D)	17. (B)	18. (D)	19. (C)	20. (D)
21. (B)	22. (C)	23. (D)	24. (C)	25. (A)					

HOTS (ACHIEVERS SECTION)

26. (C)	27. (C)	28. (D)	29. (B)	30. (C)

7. WEATHER AND SKY

Answer Key

1. (A)	2. (A)	3. (B)	4. (A)	5. (B)	6. (C)	7. (A)	8. (C)	9. (B)	10. (D)
11. (C)	12. (A)	13. (D)	14. (B)	15. (A)	16. (B)	17. (C)	18. (D)	19. (B)	20. (D)
21. (B)	22. (C)	23. (B)	24. (B)	25. (D)					

26. (B)	27. (A)	28. (D)	29. (B)	30. (B)

9. LOGICAL REASONING

Answer Key

1. (D)	2. (B)	3. (D)	4. (B)	5. (D)	6. (B)	7. (A)	8. (D)	9. (B)	10. (B)
11. (D)	12. (A)	13. (B)	14. (D)	15. (A)	16. (A)	17. (A)	18. (A)	19. (D)	20. (B)
21. (C)	22. (D)	23. (A)	24. (B)	25. (A)	26. (B)	27. (A)	28. (D)	29. (A)	30. (D)
31. (B)	32. (C)	33. (C)	34. (A)	35. (B)					

1. **(D)**
   Pattern followed in the given series is:
   $428 - 10 = 418 \rightarrow 418 + 12 = 430$….. so on..

2. **(B)**
   $9 \times 5 = 45$, and $7 \times 6 = 42$

3. **(D)**
   Every number is multiplied by 3.

4. **(B)**
   Every third figure is a triangle after the first triangle.

5. **(D)**
   Pattern followed: coloured corners in clockwise direction.

10. **(B)**
   Except (b) all the other options have a smaller shape inserted into a bigger shape.

11. **(D)**
   Snake, Turtle, Lizard, and crocodile are reptiles.

12. **(A)**
   Counting of straight lines in the figures.

13. **(B)**
   Two similar shapes are overlapped on each other.

14. **(D)**
   The figures are divided into eight equal parts.

15. **(A)**
   The right-most figure enlarges and becomes the outer figure and the second and the third figure gets placed over each other.

26. **(B)**
   Pen is lightest.

27. **(A)**
   Bottle has least capacity.

28. **(D)**
   Pen is lighter than book.

30. **(D)**
   Spider S is farthest to the ladder.

Answer Key

1. (B)	2. (C)	3. (B)	4. (A)	5. (C)	6. (A)	7. (C)	8. (A)	9. (B)	10. (B)
11. (A)	12. (D)	13. (D)	14. (B)	15. (D)	16. (C)	17. (C)	18. (A)	19. (D)	20. (A)
21. (D)	22. (C)	23. (B)	24. (B)	25. (B)	26. (D)	27. (D)	28. (C)	29. (A)	30. (B)
31. (A)	32. (D)	33. (D)	34. (C)	35. (B)					

SAMPLE OMR ANSWER SHEET

1. STUDENT NAME (IN ENGLISH CAPITAL LETTERS ONLY)

Students must write and darken the respective circles completely using HB Pencil only. Othewise their Answer Sheets will not be evaluated.

PERSONAL DETAILS

2. SCHOOL CODE

3. CLASS

4. SECTION

5. ROLL NO.

6. QUESTION PAPER SET

A ○
B ○
C ○
D ○

7. MOBILE NUMBER

8. GENDER

MALE ○

FEMALE ○

9. STREAM
(Only for Class XI and XII Students)

MATHEMATICS ○
BIOLOGY ○
OTHERS ○

MARK YOUR ANSWERS

No.					No.				
1.	Ⓐ	Ⓑ	Ⓒ	Ⓓ	26.	Ⓐ	Ⓑ	Ⓒ	Ⓓ
2.	Ⓐ	Ⓑ	Ⓒ	Ⓓ	27.	Ⓐ	Ⓑ	Ⓒ	Ⓓ
3.	Ⓐ	Ⓑ	Ⓒ	Ⓓ	28.	Ⓐ	Ⓑ	Ⓒ	Ⓓ
4.	Ⓐ	Ⓑ	Ⓒ	Ⓓ	29.	Ⓐ	Ⓑ	Ⓒ	Ⓓ
5.	Ⓐ	Ⓑ	Ⓒ	Ⓓ	30.	Ⓐ	Ⓑ	Ⓒ	Ⓓ
6.	Ⓐ	Ⓑ	Ⓒ	Ⓓ	31.	Ⓐ	Ⓑ	Ⓒ	Ⓓ
7.	Ⓐ	Ⓑ	Ⓒ	Ⓓ	32.	Ⓐ	Ⓑ	Ⓒ	Ⓓ
8.	Ⓐ	Ⓑ	Ⓒ	Ⓓ	33.	Ⓐ	Ⓑ	Ⓒ	Ⓓ
9.	Ⓐ	Ⓑ	Ⓒ	Ⓓ	34.	Ⓐ	Ⓑ	Ⓒ	Ⓓ
10.	Ⓐ	Ⓑ	Ⓒ	Ⓓ	35.	Ⓐ	Ⓑ	Ⓒ	Ⓓ
11.	Ⓐ	Ⓑ	Ⓒ	Ⓓ	36.	Ⓐ	Ⓑ	Ⓒ	Ⓓ
12.	Ⓐ	Ⓑ	Ⓒ	Ⓓ	37.	Ⓐ	Ⓑ	Ⓒ	Ⓓ
13.	Ⓐ	Ⓑ	Ⓒ	Ⓓ	38.	Ⓐ	Ⓑ	Ⓒ	Ⓓ
14.	Ⓐ	Ⓑ	Ⓒ	Ⓓ	39.	Ⓐ	Ⓑ	Ⓒ	Ⓓ
15.	Ⓐ	Ⓑ	Ⓒ	Ⓓ	40.	Ⓐ	Ⓑ	Ⓒ	Ⓓ
16.	Ⓐ	Ⓑ	Ⓒ	Ⓓ	41.	Ⓐ	Ⓑ	Ⓒ	Ⓓ
17.	Ⓐ	Ⓑ	Ⓒ	Ⓓ	42.	Ⓐ	Ⓑ	Ⓒ	Ⓓ
18.	Ⓐ	Ⓑ	Ⓒ	Ⓓ	43.	Ⓐ	Ⓑ	Ⓒ	Ⓓ
19.	Ⓐ	Ⓑ	Ⓒ	Ⓓ	44.	Ⓐ	Ⓑ	Ⓒ	Ⓓ
20.	Ⓐ	Ⓑ	Ⓒ	Ⓓ	45.	Ⓐ	Ⓑ	Ⓒ	Ⓓ
21.	Ⓐ	Ⓑ	Ⓒ	Ⓓ	46.	Ⓐ	Ⓑ	Ⓒ	Ⓓ
22.	Ⓐ	Ⓑ	Ⓒ	Ⓓ	47.	Ⓐ	Ⓑ	Ⓒ	Ⓓ
23.	Ⓐ	Ⓑ	Ⓒ	Ⓓ	48.	Ⓐ	Ⓑ	Ⓒ	Ⓓ
24.	Ⓐ	Ⓑ	Ⓒ	Ⓓ	49.	Ⓐ	Ⓑ	Ⓒ	Ⓓ
25.	Ⓐ	Ⓑ	Ⓒ	Ⓓ	50.	Ⓐ	Ⓑ	Ⓒ	Ⓓ

Signature of the Student & Date of Examination

Signature of the Invigilator & Date of Examination